HSC
Health & Safety Commission

Health and safety at quarries

Quarries Regulations 1999

APPROVED CODE OF PRACTICE
L118

HSE BOOKS

Approved Code of Practice

This Code has been approved by the Health and Safety Commission, with the consent of the Secretary of State. It gives practical advice on how to comply with the law. If you follow the advice you will be doing enough to comply with the law in respect of those specific matters on which the Code gives advice. You may use alternative methods to those set out in the Code in order to comply with the law.

However the Code has a special legal status. If you are prosecuted for breach of health and safety law, and it is proved that you did not follow the relevant provisions of the Code, you will need to show that you have complied with the law in some other way or a court will find you at fault.

Guidance

This guidance is issued by the Health and Safety Commission. Following the guidance is not compulsory and you are free to take other action. But if you do follow the guidance you will normally be doing enough to comply with the law. Health and safety inspectors seek to secure compliance with the law and may refer to this guidance as illustrating good practice.

Contents

By virtue of Section 16(1) of the Health and Safety at Work etc Act 1974, and with the consent of the Secretary of State for the Environment, Transport and the Regions, the Health and Safety Commission has on 25 May 1999 approved the Code of Practice entitled *Health and safety at quarries*.

The Code of Practice is approved for the purposes of providing practical guidance with respect to the requirements of the Quarries Regulations 1999. The Code of Practice comes into force on 1 January 2000.

Reference in this Code of Practice to another document does not imply approval by HSC of that document except to the extent necessary to give effect to this Code of Practice.

Signed

ROSEMARY BANNER
Secretary to the Health and Safety Commission

10 August 1999

Preface

The Quarries Regulations 1999 were made under the Health and Safety at Work etc Act 1974 and come into force on 1 January 2000. The Regulations apply to all quarries. The full text of the Quarries Regulations 1999[1] can be obtained from the Stationery Office.

This document contains an Approved Code of Practice (ACOP) and guidance on the duties in the Quarries Regulations 1999.

The text of the Regulations is in italic type. The accompanying ACOP material, which has the status described on the cover page, is in bold type and additional guidance is in normal type. Footnotes and appendices are guidance material unless explicitly stated.

1 The Quarries Regulations 1999 are intended to protect the health and safety of people working at a quarry and others who may be affected by quarrying activities. They apply to both employees and the self-employed. They are also intended to safeguard people not working at the quarry (eg those living, passing or working nearby, or visiting, for example to buy materials).*

2 It is important to remember that a legal duty under one of these regulations can not be passed on to someone else by means of a contract. For example an operator who appoints a contractor as explosives supervisor still has the ultimate legal responsibility under regulation 25 to ensure that explosives work is carried out safely.

3 Other health and safety legislation also applies to quarry work. These Regulations do not relieve anyone of their duties under such legislation. The most relevant legislation is listed in Table 1.

Table 1 Legislation relevant to quarry work

Title	Summary
Health and Safety at Work etc Act 1974[2]	General duties to ensure health and safety of employees and others so far as is reasonably practicable
Management of Health and Safety at Work Regulations 1999[3]	General management of health and safety including availability of health and safety advice and risk assessment
Provision and Use of Work Equipment Regulations 1998[4]	Machinery, vehicle and other work equipment suitability and safety
Control of Substances Hazardous Health Regulations 1999[5]	Control of health risks
Workplace (Health, Safety and Welfare) Regulations 1992[6]	General workplace issues, inside and out including traffic routes and prevention of falls
Manual Handling Operations Regulations 1992[7]	Control of risks from handling heavy and awkward loads
Personal Protective Equipment at Work Regulations 1992[8]	Provision and use of personal protective equipment
Noise at Work Regulations 1989[9]	Control of exposure to noise
Confined Spaces Regulations 1997[10]	Safe working in confined spaces, ie where there is a risk of death or serious injury from hazardous substances or dangerous conditions (eg lack of oxygen)
Lifting Operations and Lifting Equipment Regulations 1998[11]	Requirements regarding the use of lifting equipment
Reporting of Injuries, Diseases and Dangerous Occurrences Regulations 1995[12]	Duties to report accidents, diseases and dangerous occurrences

* Other specific legislation will take precedence in some cases. This includes the Road Traffic Act 1988 for vehicles on public roads and the Environment Protection Act 1990 for off-site dust, noise and vibration.

Part I Interpretation and general

Regulation 1

Citation and commencement

(1) These Regulations may be cited as the Quarries Regulations 1999 and subject to paragraphs (2) and (3) shall come into force on 1 January 2000.

(2) Regulation 32, with the exception of paragraph (4), shall come into force on 1 January 2001 with respect to any tip which was not a classified tip for the purposes of regulation 2(1) of the 1971 Regulations.

(3) Regulation 32(4) shall come into force on 1 January 2002 with respect to any notifiable tip which was not a classified tip for the purposes of regulation 2(1) of the 1971 Regulations.

4   The requirements relating to appraisal and geotechnical assessment of excavations and tips come into force later than the rest of these Regulations. The effect of this is to give one year for appraisals and two years for geotechnical assessments to be completed. This delay does not apply to the other requirements relating to the safety of excavations and tips which come into force immediately.

5   For tips which were classified under the previous legislation, the appraisal and geotechnical assessment requirements come into force at the same time as the other regulations. These tips were previously subject to routine assessment and, in practice, the new requirements are similar.

Regulation 2

Interpretation

(1) In these Regulations, unless the context otherwise requires -

"the 1954 Act" means the Mines and Quarries Act 1954;[a]

"the 1969 Act" means the Mines and Quarries (Tips) Act 1969;[b]

"the 1971 Regulations" means the Mines and Quarries (Tips) Regulations 1971;[c]

"the 1999 Regulations" means the Management of Health and Safety at Work Regulations 1999;[d]

"appoint" in relation to a person means appoint in writing with a written statement summarising his duties and authority, and "appointed" shall be construed accordingly;

"competent" in relation to a person means a person with sufficient training, experience, knowledge and other qualities to enable him properly to undertake the duties assigned to him, and "competence" shall be construed accordingly;

"detonator" means an initiator for explosives that contains a charge of high explosive fired by means of a flame, spark, electric current or shock tube;

[a] 1954 c.70, extended by the Mines and Quarries (Tips) Act 1969 (c.10) and the Mines Management Act 1971 (c.20): relevant amending instruments are SI 1974/2013, 1976/2063, 1993/1897.
[b] 1969 c.10 to which there are amendments not relevant to these Regulations.
[c] SI 1971/1377.
[d] SI 1992/2051; amended by SI 1994/2865, 1997/135, 1997/1840.

"excavation" means any place at the quarry where minerals are or have been extracted and includes the ground, faces or sides of the quarry and any other incline;

"excavations and tips rules" means the rules referred to at regulation 31;

"the Executive" means the Health and Safety Executive;

"exploder" means a device designed for firing detonators;

"explosives" means explosive articles or explosive substances both as defined in the Classification and Labelling of Explosives Regulations 1983;[(a)]

"explosives store" means -

    (a)   premises registered in accordance with section 21 of the Explosives Act 1875[(b)] ("the 1875 Act");

    (b)   a magazine licensed in accordance with sections 6 to 8 of the 1875 Act; or

    (c)   a store licensed in accordance with section 15 of the 1875 Act;

"geotechnical assessment" has the meaning given to it in regulation 33(1);

"geotechnical specialist" means a chartered engineer or chartered geologist who has -

    (a)   three or more years relevant experience in soil mechanics, rock mechanics or excavation engineering; and

    (b)   is competent to perform a geotechnical analysis to determine the hazard and risk arising from the excavation or tip being assessed;

"hazard" in relation to an excavation or tip means having the potential to cause harm to the health and safety of any person;

"health and safety document" shall be construed in accordance with regulation 7;

"maintained" with respect to the quarry and its plant means maintained, where necessary to secure the health and safety of any person, in an efficient state, in efficient working order and in good repair, and *"maintenance"* shall be construed accordingly;

"management structure" shall be construed in accordance with regulation 8;

"mine" means any mine within the meaning of the 1954 Act;

"minerals" includes stone, slate, clay, gravel, sand and other natural deposits except peat;

"misfire" means an occurrence in relation to the firing of shots where -

    (a)   testing before firing reveals broken continuity which cannot be rectified; or

    (b)   a shot or any part of a shot fails to explode when an attempt is made to fire it;

(a) SI 1983/1140; amended by SI 1987/605, 1996/2093.
(b) 1875 c.17; the relevant amending instruments are SI 1974/1885, 1984/510, 1987/52.

"notifiable excavation" and "notifiable tip" shall be construed in accordance with regulation 34(3);

"operator" in relation to a quarry means the person in overall control of the working of the quarry;

"preparation for sale" includes the crushing, screening, washing, drying and bagging of minerals;

"public road" means (in England and Wales) a highway maintainable at public expense within the meaning of section 329 of the Highways Act 1980[a] and (in Scotland) a public road within the meaning assigned to that term by section 151 of the Roads (Scotland) Act 1984;[b]

"quarry" has the meaning given to it by regulation 3;

"railway company" means any person authorised by an enactment to construct, work or carry on a railway and for the purposes of this definition the expression "enactment" includes a provision of an order or scheme made under or confirmed by an Act;

"safety fuse" means a flexible cord that contains an internal burning medium by which fire is conveyed at a continuous and uniform rate for the purpose of firing plain detonators or blackpowder, without initiating burning in a similar fuse that may be in lateral contact alongside;

"shot" means a single shot or a series of shots fired as part of one blast;

"shotfirer" means a person appointed pursuant to regulation 25(2)(a)(ii) to be responsible for shotfiring operations;

"shotfiring operations" includes -

(a)   checking to ensure that the blasting specification is still appropriate for the site conditions at the time the blasting is to take place;

(b)   mixing explosives;

(c)   priming a cartridge;

(d)   charging and stemming a shothole;

(e)   linking or connecting a round of shots;

(f)   withdrawal and sheltering of persons;

(g)   inspecting and testing a shotfiring circuit;

(h)   firing a shot; and

(i)   checking for misfires;

"tip" means an accumulation or deposit of any substance at a quarry (whether in a solid or liquid state or in solution or suspension) and includes, but is not limited to, overburden dumps, backfill, spoil heaps, stock piles and lagoons, and where any wall or other structure retains or confines a tip then it shall be deemed to form part of the tip;

(a) 1980 c.66 to which there are amendments not relevant to these Regulations.
(b) 1984 c.54.

"*trainee shotfirer*" means a person appointed pursuant to regulation 25(2)(a)(ii) to undergo training in shotfiring operations under the close personal supervision of a shotfirer;

"*vehicle*" means any mechanically propelled vehicle (including mechanically propelled plant);

"*vehicles rules*" means the rules referred to at regulation 14.

(2) Unless the context otherwise requires, any reference in these Regulations to -

(a) a numbered regulation or Schedule is a reference to the regulation or Schedule in these Regulations so numbered;

(b) a numbered paragraph is a reference to the paragraph so numbered in the regulation or Schedule in which that reference occurs; and

(c) any specified document shall operate as a reference to that document as revised or reissued from time to time.

Meaning of quarry

(1) In these Regulations "*quarry*" means -

(a) subject to paragraph (2), an excavation or system of excavations made for the purpose of, or in connection with, the extraction of minerals (whether in their natural state or in solution or suspension) or products of minerals, being neither a mine nor merely a well or borehole or a well and borehole combined;

(b) any reclamation site (and for this purpose "*reclamation site*" means a site where the extraction of minerals forms part of the process whereby that site is restored for agricultural, industrial or domestic use) from which minerals are being extracted for sale or further use; or

(c) any disused tip which is not at a mine being worked within the meaning of regulation 2(3) of the Management and Administration of Safety and Health at Mines Regulations 1993[a] from which minerals are being extracted for sale or further use.

(2) Notwithstanding paragraph (1)(a), in these Regulations "*quarry*" does not include -

(a) an excavation or system of excavations made for the purpose of or in connection with the extraction of such minerals or products of minerals where the exclusive purpose of that extraction is to enable the minerals or products of minerals so extracted to be used for the purpose of carrying out any building, civil engineering or engineering construction work on the site at which the extraction has taken place;

(b) a public road; or

(c) a railway line which is exclusively under the control of -

(i) a railway company, or

(a) SI 1993/1897; amended by SI 1995/2005, 1996/1592.

(ii)   a person who carries on an undertaking which consists of, or the main activity or one of the main activities of which consists of, the management of a network within the meaning of subsection (1) of section 83 of the Railways Act 1993.[a]

(3)   For the purposes of these Regulations, the following shall be deemed to form part of a quarry -

(a)   so much of the surface (including buildings, structures and works thereon) surrounding or adjacent to the quarry as is occupied for the purpose of, or in connection with -

(i)   the working of the quarry,

(ii)   the consumption, use, storage or preparation for sale of the minerals or products thereof extracted from the quarry, or

(iii)   the removal from the quarry of any substance extracted from the quarry; and

(b)   any tip -

(i)   for the time being used in conjunction or connection with the operation of the quarry, or

(ii)   subject to paragraph (4)(a) (whether or not it is for the time being in use) situated on premises occupied by the operator of the quarry;

(4)   For the purposes of these Regulations, where

(a)   a tip is for the time being used in conjunction or connection with the operation of two or more quarries and is situated on premises occupied exclusively by the operator of one of those quarries, it shall be treated as forming part of that quarry unless -

(i)   the operator of one of the other quarries in conjunction or connection with which the tip is for the time being used has agreed that the tip should be treated as forming part of the quarry of which he is the operator, and

(ii)   notice to that effect has been given to the Executive by that operator;

(b)   a tip is for the time being used in conjunction or connection with the operation of two or more quarries and is situated on premises occupied jointly by the operators of two or more of those quarries, the last-named operators shall, for the purposes of these Regulations, be treated as being in joint and several control of that tip and as being jointly and severally responsible therefore unless -

(i)   the said operators have agreed that one of their number should be treated as being in control of that tip and responsible therefore, and

(ii)   notice to that effect has been given to the Executive by the operator who is to be so treated;

(5)   Upon receipt of a notice given in accordance with paragraphs (4)(a)(ii) or (4)(b)(ii), the tip named in that notice shall be treated as forming part of the quarry specified in the said notice.

3

(a) 1993 c.43.

Application

(1)   Subject to paragraph (2) and save where the contrary intention appears, these Regulations shall apply to all quarries where persons work.

(2)   These Regulations shall not apply to any -

(a)   quarry at which there has been no extraction or preparation for sale of minerals within the previous 12 months;

(b)   quarry in relation to which notice of abandonment or ceasing of operations has been given to the Executive in accordance with regulation 45(1), provided that the quarry is no longer being used for the extraction or preparation for sale of minerals; or

(c)   part of a quarry which is being used exclusively by a person for a work activity unconnected with -

(i)   the extraction of minerals, or

(ii)   the preparation for sale of minerals,

provided that no work activity set out in paragraph (3) is being carried on at that quarry.

(3)   The work activities mentioned in paragraph (2) are any work carried on -

(a)   with a view to abandoning that quarry; or

(b)   for the purpose of preventing the flow from that quarry into an adjacent quarry of water or material that flows when wet.

(4)   These Regulations shall apply to a self-employed person as they apply to an employer and as if that self-employed person were both an employer and a person at work.

6   Regulation 3 defines 'quarry' as used in these Regulations; regulation 4 explains what activities in a quarry are covered by these Regulations. For simplicity the guidance on these matters has been combined.

What is a quarry?

7   A quarry includes:

(a)   all the surface mineral workings;

(b)   tips (even if they are outside the site boundary);

(c)   storage of minerals, including stockpiles;

(d)   areas used for the preparation of extracted materials for sale (this includes crushing, screening, washing, drying and bagging);

(e)   the buildings and structures at the quarry that are used for the working of the quarry;

(f)   common areas (for example quarry roadways and railways, but not public roads or railways under the control of a rail company); and

(g)   sites where prospecting with a view to the extraction of minerals is carried out - where this is not covered by the Borehole Sites and Operations Regulations 1995.[13]

What activities in a quarry are covered?

8   These Regulations only apply to quarries:

(a)   being prepared for extraction of minerals (this includes coal);

(b)   where mineral extraction or preparation takes place as part of a work activity;

(c)   where work to prevent water or other material flowing into an adjacent quarry takes place - even after quarrying has finished; and

(d)   being prepared for abandonment, for example landscaping.

9   Where a quarry is no longer used for the extraction of minerals and the Health and Safety Executive (HSE) has been notified in accordance with regulation 45, these Regulations do not apply, but the site must be left in a safe condition when quarrying work finishes (regulation 6(4)).

Demarcation

10   Dividing a quarry into areas where these Regulations apply and other areas where they do not, may, in some cases, cause confusion. In such cases the operator may find it more convenient to treat the whole quarry site as being subject to these Regulations.

11   Areas to which these Regulations do not apply, in the opinion of the operator, should be clearly marked on a site plan (see regulation 7(2)(c)). This should not include any areas or activities described in paragraph 7. This plan will form part of the health and safety document. The arrangements for co-ordinating health and safety between the operator and the occupants of excluded areas should be explained in the health and safety document. The plan and arrangements should be subject to review in the same way as the rest of the health and safety document.

Excavations associated with construction work

12   These Regulations do not cover excavations made:

(a)   solely for the purpose of carrying out any building, civil engineering or engineering construction work; and

(b)   where the minerals or products of minerals extracted are used on the site at which the extraction has taken place.

13   These Regulations will not apply where minerals are extracted from excavations (for example borrow pits or cuttings) during civil engineering contracts, as an integral part of a construction project, and that material is used in the same project (see regulation 3(2)(a)).

14   These Regulations will, however, apply where materials are extracted for sale or use away from the site of extraction. For example, if sand or gravel is excavated away from the line of a roadway that is being constructed, the extraction site will be a quarry as defined.

Reclamation sites etc

15   These Regulations apply to sites while minerals are extracted for sale or further use as part of another process, such as reclamation. For example, coal might be recovered to offset the costs of landscaping a tip.

Tips

16   Tips used in conjunction or connection with the operation of a quarry are covered by these Regulations, even if they are some distance from the excavation. This is the case whether the tip is only used for waste or landscaping material or is, for example, a clay stockpile adjacent to a brickworks. Stockpiled material which is not used in conjunction or connection with the operation of a quarry, for example that which has been sold and is stored at the customer's premises, is not covered by these Regulations.

17   Where quarries use the same tip, the operators should agree which of them is responsible for the safe operation of the tip. This should normally be the operator who is in the best position to manage the tipping operations. If a tip is clearly within one of the quarries then this is normally the operator of that quarry. Where no operator has accepted responsibility, and notified HSE accordingly, all the operators who use the tip are individually responsible for its safe operation.

Rail lines

18   A railway which is operated by a railway company or by the manager of a railway network (such as Railtrack) is not legally part of the quarry. However, any part of a railway system which a quarry runs itself does form part of the quarry.

19   For example, the sidings at a quarry may be run by the quarry, but the rail link to the main line may be operated by a railway company. In this case the sidings would be the responsibility of the quarry operator and the line linking the quarry to the main line would be the responsibility of the railway company.

20   Some of the requirements in the Railway Safety (Miscellaneous Provisions) Regulations 1997[14] apply at quarries. The Railways (Safety Case) Regulations 1994[15] apply to lines which are not legally part of the quarry.

Temporary closure

21   HSE does not need to be formally notified of temporary closure of quarries lasting up to 12 months. It is, however, helpful if quarry operators advise the local inspector in these circumstances. HSE must be notified of quarries that are abandoned or suspended for periods of more than a year.

Regulation 5

Duties of the person entitled to work the quarry

(1)   The person entitled to work a quarry shall not permit another person to be the operator of that quarry unless that person is suitable and has sufficient resources to be able to operate the quarry safely.

(2)   Where the person entitled to work a quarry permits another person to be the operator of that quarry, he shall make a written record of that permission which record shall be signed by the person so entitled and the operator and a copy of which shall be provided to the operator.

(3)   The said record and copy shall be kept by the person so entitled and the operator respectively for the duration of the said permission.

(4)   The person so entitled shall provide the operator with any relevant information available to him which might affect the health and safety of persons at work at the quarry.

22   The term 'operator' is defined in regulation 2. It is the 'person' (a legal term which can mean individual or company) who is in overall control of the quarry. Most of the duties under these Regulations fall on the operator.

23   If the person entitled to work the quarry does so, he/she is the operator. In any other circumstances, he/she must appoint the operator, normally a company, in writing.

24   There may be more than one person entitled to work a site. In this case they should either reach agreement that there will be one operator in overall control, or the site should be divided into clearly defined areas, each area being a separate quarry with its own operator.

25   Where the person entitled to work the quarry agrees that someone else will operate the quarry, he/she must be satisfied that the proposed operator has enough resources to enable the quarry to be worked safely, such as enough experienced and, where necessary, qualified staff. The agreement must be recorded in writing and both parties must have a copy. In most cases of this type there will be a written contract setting out the agreement and this would form a suitable record. Both parties must keep copies of the agreement while it remains in force.

26   The person entitled to work the quarry must also pass to the operator any information relevant to working the quarry safely, for example geological information, geotechnical reports, details of previous mine or quarry workings and information about materials deposited on the site.

27   It is important that everybody who works at a quarry knows who the operator is, who manages the quarry and how they can be contacted. This can be achieved by displaying a notice at a suitable place at the quarry setting out the operator's name, the management structure and relevant addresses and telephone numbers.

28   If the person entitled to work the quarry retains some control over the way the quarry is worked, for example by the terms of the contract, he/she may still have some duties under the Health and Safety at Work etc Act 1974 (HSW Act), particularly sections 3 and 4.

29   Such control might, for example, exist in a coal quarry where the person entitled to work the quarry specifies the excavation and coaling limits of excavation (coaling lines). These limits must be set so that the coal can be removed safely and that the finished excavation will be safe.

30   Where the person entitled to work a quarry does not do so, but undertakes another work activity there, such as supervision of coal cleaning operations, he/she has a duty to comply with the relevant statutory provisions which apply to those activities.

31   The owner of a disused tip at an abandoned quarry is responsible for its safety, as explained in Part II of the Mines and Quarries (Tips) Act 1969. To carry out these responsibilities, he/she will need certain information after the quarry is abandoned, for example reports of geotechnical assessment.

Regulation 6

General duties of the operator

(1)   It shall be the duty of the operator of every quarry to take the necessary measures to ensure, so far as is reasonably practicable, that the quarry and its plant are designed, constructed, equipped, commissioned, operated and maintained in such a way that persons at work can perform the work assigned to them without endangering their own health and safety or the health and safety of others.

(2)   The operator shall co-ordinate the implementation of all measures relating to the health and safety of persons at work at the quarry.

(3)   Without prejudice to the generality of paragraph (1), where necessary to ensure the health and safety of any person the operator shall ensure that any building (whether temporary or permanent) or structure -

(a)   is designed, constructed, erected, operated, supervised and maintained so as to withstand any reasonably foreseeable environmental forces; and

(b)   has a construction and solidity which is appropriate to the nature of its use.

(4)   The operator shall ensure that in the event of the abandonment of or ceasing of operations at a quarry, the quarry is left, so far as is reasonably practicable, in a safe condition.

32   Regulation 6 is the underpinning requirement of these Regulations. It is intended to secure a co-ordinated, proactive approach to the management of health and safety, which ensures that risks are properly controlled.

33   The distinctive and key duty of the operator, normally the company running the quarry, is to manage health and safety for the whole site, including work carried out by contractors. Operators have overall responsibility for planning, co-ordinating and overseeing work.

34   The operator should, therefore, ensure that contractors have correctly identified hazards and control measures by carrying out risk assessments under regulation 3 of the Management of Health and Safety at Work Regulations 1999, and other relevant legislation (see Table 1).

35 To meet the duty in regulation 6(1), the operator needs to consider:

(a) the geotechnical features of the site;

(b) the proximity of homes, roads, footpaths, bridleways, schools and other areas where the public are likely to be found (including any likely future development);

(c) the presence of water courses, services (particularly any overhead electric power lines), disused mine or quarry workings;

(d) the use, width, condition and inclination of traffic routes, taking account of pedestrian safety (see Appendix 4, paragraph 18) and the type of mobile plant to be used;

(e) the siting and building of tips, including stockpiles, lagoons and related structures, and their stability;

(f) the risks to health from the materials being worked (eg silica content) and the working methods;

(g) the plant (fixed or mobile) that is required;

(h) the safe use and maintenance of plant and machinery; and

(i) the safe use of explosives.

36 Using this information, and that from the various risk assessments and the design of the excavation (see regulation 30) the operator can plan how the quarry should be equipped, managed and worked. The plan should be reviewed as the quarry develops and in the event of significant changes or new information about the risks (see also regulations 7 and 11).

37 The proper planning of a quarry will not eliminate all health and safety risks, but it can make a major contribution. The remaining risks should be tackled at source wherever possible, with priority being given to measures that safeguard the maximum number of people.

Public safety

38 There are public safety implications in many of the points in paragraph 35, but the operator should also consider more broadly ways in which working the quarry may create a risk to the public. The use of explosives and any public access to the site are obvious examples.

39 Members of the public in a quarry are likely to be exposed to significant risks. From a health and safety point of view, it is normally better if public rights of way are diverted around quarries. Where diversion is not possible, precautions must be implemented based on a detailed risk assessment of the route and the area around it. The precautions must be reviewed regularly in the light of experience.

Co-ordination, communication and co-operation

40 Regulation 11 of the Management of Health and Safety at Work Regulations 1999 requires all employers sharing a workplace to work together to ensure health and safety. Regulation 6(2) of the Quarries Regulations 1999 requires the operator to take the initiative in this matter.

41 Many quarries have employees from several companies, as well as self-employed workers, on site for some or all of the time. For example, delivery

drivers are present for short periods; others, such as blasting contractors, form an essential part of the extraction process. The operator is responsible for the co-ordination of the work of all these people.

Employers and self-employed contractors

42   Irrespective of the duties of the operator under these Regulations, each contractor remains responsible for complying with other relevant health and safety legislation (see regulation 41). A list of the most relevant health and safety law is provided in Table 1.

43   The primary duties under most of this other legislation rest on the employer or self-employed contractor.* Quarry operators do not need to repeat work done by others to carry out their duties, but should satisfy themselves that systems are in place to ensure, so far as is reasonably practicable, the health and safety of everybody in, or near, the quarry and that these systems work in practice.

44   Construction and civil engineering work, excluding the construction of excavations or tips carried out as part of mineral extraction at an active quarry, is subject to the Construction (Health, Safety and Welfare) Regulations 1996.[16] The Construction (Design and Management) Regulations 1994[17] also place particular responsibilities on various parties including clients, developers, designers and principal contractors.

45   Although the majority of the duties under these Regulations are placed on the operator, contractors may also be legally liable if, by their act or default, they cause the operator to commit an offence (see section 36(1) of the HSW Act).

Design and construction of buildings and structures

46   Buildings and man-made structures in quarries, for example hoppers, storage bins and conveyor systems, need to be designed and constructed to normal structural standards, unless there are local factors which mean that higher standards are required.

Maintenance

47   The quarry, including its plant, buildings, and structures, must be sufficiently maintained to ensure, so far as reasonably practicable, the safety of everyone working there or immediately affected. This can be achieved using the written scheme required under regulation 12.

* Sometimes additional duties are placed on people who are, to any extent, in control of workplaces or work equipment. Examples of this are the HSW Act section 4 and the Provision and Use of Work Equipment Regulations 1998 (see regulation 3(3)(b)). The operator and a contractor may therefore both have legal duties relating to the same equipment.

The health and safety document

(1)   The operator shall ensure that no work is carried out at the quarry unless a document (in these Regulations referred to as the "health and safety document") has been prepared which -

(a)   demonstrates that the risks to which persons at work at the quarry are exposed have been assessed in accordance with regulation 3 of the 1999 Regulations;

13

(b) demonstrates that adequate measures, including measures concerning the design, use and maintenance of the quarry and of its plant, will be taken to safeguard the health and safety of persons -

    (i) at the quarry, and

    (ii) in the area immediately surrounding the quarry who are directly affected by the activities of the quarry;

(c) includes a statement of how the measures referred to in sub-paragraph (b) will be co-ordinated;

(d) gives details of the management structure and sets out the authority and duties of each person in the management structure; and

(e) records the following information -

    (i) the rules required by regulation 10(1)(a),

    (ii) the arrangements for the review of safety measures in accordance with regulation 11,

    (iii) details of the inspection, maintenance and testing schemes prepared in accordance with regulation 12,

    (iv) the rules controlling risks from vehicles required by regulation 14,

    (v) details of the permit to work system required by regulation 18,

    (vi) the shotfiring rules required by regulation 25(2),

    (vii) the excavations and tips rules required by regulation 31,

    (viii) the conclusions of any appraisal or assessment of an excavation or tip undertaken in accordance with regulation 32, and

    (ix) the arrangements for health surveillance required by regulation 43.

(2) In addition to the matters referred to in paragraph (1), the health and safety document shall where appropriate also include -

(a) a plan detailing the equipment and measures required to protect persons at work at the quarry from the risk of explosion;

(b) where toxic gases are or may be present in the atmosphere at the quarry in such concentration that the atmosphere may be harmful to the health of persons at work, a plan detailing the protective equipment and measures required to protect persons at work at the quarry from the harmful atmosphere; and

(c) a diagram of the quarry indicating those areas to which these Regulations do not apply by virtue of regulation 4(2)(c).

(3) The operator shall ensure that the health and safety document, including any information recorded therein pursuant to paragraph (1)(e), is -

(a) kept up to date; and

(b) made available to each employer of persons at work at the quarry and to all persons at work at the quarry.

(4)   The operator shall ensure -

(a)   that the measures identified in the health and safety document are taken; and

(b)   that any plans included in that document are followed.

(5)   Each person in the management structure shall carry out the duties assigned to him in the health and safety document so as to protect the health and safety of persons at work at the quarry.

48   Every quarry must have a health and safety document, irrespective of the number of employees. It should be written so that the relevant parts can be easily understood by all those on whom it places responsibilities.

49   Each existing quarry should already have a health and safety document, as it was a requirement of the Quarries Miscellaneous Health and Safety Provisions Regulations 1995. This document needs to be reviewed to ensure that it meets all the new requirements.

50   The health and safety document must be drawn up before work starts. Preparation, in the case of a new quarry, should begin at the design stage. It should be continuously developed to keep it up to date as more is learned about the geology of the site, or as management systems or working methods change.

51   To be any use, the health and safety document must be a living document providing practical information to people at the quarry about health and safety measures and their role in implementing them. Glossy documentation, produced by an outside consultant, which is only ever used to try to satisfy an inspector is a waste of time and money. The systematic processes and the involvement of the workforce which are needed to produce an effective document can be as valuable as the finished document.

52   In most cases the health and safety document will not be a single document, but a collection of documents. Existing material does not need to be rewritten as long as all the requirements are addressed, and the composite document is properly cross-referenced and indexed.

53   The document must set out the management structure (see regulation 8) and explain each person's authority and the duties of those in that structure. This needs to include relevant off-site staff, such as area managers, engineers, surveyors and geologists. Where managerial responsibilities are given to subcontracted staff, they must also be included in the structure.

54   The level of detail recorded should be in proportion to the degree of risk and complexity of the organisation. Small quarries probably need only simple documentation, while large quarries are likely to need something more detailed.

55   The document must contain enough information to demonstrate that the risks have been properly assessed, and that adequate measures have been taken to safeguard the health and safety of people at work at the quarry and others who might be affected.

Contents of health and safety document

56   The information to be included in the health and safety document is, generally, at the level of schemes, procedures and arrangements rather than

detail such as the findings of the inspections. Where relevant, this must include the topics shown in Table 2.

Table 2 Topics to include in the health and safety document

Topic	Quarries Regulations 1999
Risk assessments - including those carried out under: (a) Management of Health and Safety at Work Regulations 1999; (b) Control of Substances Hazardous to Health Regulations 1999; (c) Manual Handling Operations Regulations 1992; (d) Noise at Work Regulations 1989.	7(1)(a)
Health and safety measures	7(1)(b)
Co-ordination of safety measures	7(1)(c)
Management structure	7(1)(d) and 8
Explosion risk control plan	7(2)(a)
Toxic gas protection plan	7(2)(b)
Plan of quarry, showing where regulations do/do not apply	7(2)(c)
All instructions, rules, and schemes which apply to quarry, including:	7(1)(e)(i) and 10
Scheme for the inspection and maintenance of the quarry including excavations, tips, plant etc	12
Vehicles rules	14
Permit-to-work system	18
Shotfiring rules	25
Excavations and tips rules	31
Conclusions of appraisals and assessments of excavations and tips	32 and 33
Frequency of review of safety measures	11(b)

57 The health and safety document can also usefully include the following:

(a) the health and safety policy required under section 2(3) of the HSW Act;

(b) the risk assessment relating to the provision of barriers around the quarry (regulation 16); and

(c) the arrangements for the identification of danger areas (regulation 22).

Implementation

58 Operators must ensure that all the measures specified in the health and safety document are taken and that any plans are followed in practice. This

involves putting in place appropriate monitoring arrangements. (See regulation 11 and the guidance supporting it for information about review and monitoring.)

Provision of information

59   A copy of the health and safety document should be held on site. It must be made available to every employer and all those who work at the quarry, so that they can understand the risks and control measures relating to their work. A copy of the whole document need not be given to everybody, but everyone needs to have copies of those parts with which they have to comply.

60   It is good practice to make the parts dealing with public safety available to people living or working near the quarry.

Management structure

(1)   With a view to ensuring the health, safety and welfare of those persons identified in regulation 7(1)(b)(i) and (ii), it shall be the duty of the operator to -

(a)   establish a management structure which enables the quarry to be operated in accordance with the health and safety document;

(b)   make a record of the management structure and the extent of the authority and duties of persons in the said structure;

(c)   appoint a competent individual to take charge of the operation of the quarry at all times when persons are working in the quarry, provided that where the operator is an individual and is suitably qualified and competent he may appoint himself;

(d)   ensure that when, for whatever reason, the individual appointed in accordance with paragraph (1)(c) is not readily available, a competent individual is nominated as a substitute to hold the authority and perform the duties of the first named individual; and

(e)   ensure that a sufficient number of competent persons are appointed to manage the quarry safely.

(2)   Without prejudice to the generality of paragraph (1), the management structure shall be established to provide in particular that all persons working at the quarry come under the authority of a competent person in the management structure who shall have a duty to exercise such supervision of those persons as is appropriate to ensure the health and safety of those persons and of all others who may be affected by their activities.

(3)   The operator shall ensure that the management structure is reviewed regularly and revised where necessary and in particular if the quarry undergoes significant changes (including natural changes), extensions or conversions.

(4)   The operator shall ensure that each person who forms part of the management structure is provided with a copy of those parts of the health and safety document which describe his authority and duties.

(5)   The reference to a competent individual taking charge in paragraph (1)(c) is a reference to that individual taking charge subject to the overall control exercised by the operator.

61 The operator must set up a management structure that ensures that there is a sufficient number of competent people to manage the quarry safely.* This structure and the competencies required should meet the needs identified during the risk assessments and planning activities already referred to. It must include any subcontractors who have significant roles in the management of the quarry. The structure must be set out in writing and included in the health and safety document (see also paragraph 53).

62 A competent individual must be appointed to manage the operation of the quarry at all times when work is being undertaken. If the operator is a competent individual, he/she could also be this quarry manager. The arrangements for multi-shift systems, sick leave and holidays should be set out clearly. Everyone working at the quarry needs to know who this manager is.

63 All the workforce need to understand their responsibilities and authority in relation to health and safety. They also need to know how their responsibilities interrelate with those of others. It is normally best if the key responsibilities are summarised in the management structure with more detail being provided in individual job descriptions.

64 It is particularly important that managers and supervisors properly understand their health and safety responsibilities and authority. They must also be competent to do their job so that others are not put at risk (regulation 9). The type and degree of competence required will vary from job to job. In some cases particular qualifications are needed, for example where explosives are used.

65 The quarry management structure may be the same as that recorded in the operator's health and safety policy as required by section 2(3) of the HSW Act. If this is already recorded in enough detail, there is no need to produce another document.

66 The management structure should cover any senior managers off-site who are responsible for health and safety, as well as managers and supervisors working at the quarry. Where the operator is also the quarry manager, the management structure may be very simple. In other companies the structure may be more complex, but the structure should always make it clear where responsibilities lie.

67 Regulation 7 of the Management of Health and Safety at Work Regulations 1999 requires employers and the self-employed to appoint appropriate, competent people to help them carry out their duties under health and safety law. Operators must bear this in mind when drawing up their management structure.

68 The management structure must be reviewed routinely and, in particular, when the work or people involved change significantly, to ensure that it remains appropriate.

69 Operators need to inform the workforce about the management structure. They may do this by, for example, displaying a notice which gives the name of the operator, and the names and roles of managers, supervisors etc. Any such notice must include anyone who holds a position of responsibility, such as the explosives supervisor and shotfirer, even if he/she is not an employee of the operator.

* Booklet HSG65 *Successful health and safety management* (HSE Books 1997 ISBN 0 7176 1276 7) contains useful guidance on effective management of health and safety.

70   The legal responsibility for the overall control of the quarry rests on the operator and not the individual appointed to take charge of the site - unless that individual is the operator.

Training and competence

The operator shall ensure that no person undertakes any work at the quarry unless -

(a)   that person is either competent to do that work or he does so under the instruction and supervision of some other person who is competent to give instruction in and to supervise the doing of that work for the purpose of training him; and

(b)   a sufficient number of persons with the requisite competence to perform the tasks assigned to them are present.

71   Everyone working at the quarry must be competent for the work they are required to do. They, and their managers, need to know the limits of their competence. People working at a quarry must not undertake any work for which they are not competent - except under the careful instruction and supervision of a competent instructor.

72   Competence is defined in regulation 2. It also helps to keep in mind the NVQ (National Vocational Qualification) definition of competence: 'the ability to apply knowledge, understanding, practical and thinking skills to achieve effective performance to the standards required in employment. This involves solving problems and being sufficiently flexible to meet the changing demands'.

73   Everyone who works at a quarry must be properly trained and have appropriate experience and knowledge to enable them to do their work safely. A few will need other qualities such as management or interpersonal skills, or formal qualifications, for example geotechnical specialists, shotfirers and explosives supervisors. Management training must, where appropriate, include training in safety management, risk assessment and developing and using safe systems of work.

74   The risk assessments and occupational standards* should help to determine the health and safety competencies needed for particular jobs. By comparing the competencies needed with those which people already have, managers can determine what additional skills are required, and how these can be achieved, for example through training and coaching.

75   Care should be taken when using existing workers for training. Such training can be useful, but may also lead to bad practices and attitudes being passed on to a new generation of workers, for example concerning the use of personal protective equipment.

76   Health and safety training is an important way of developing competence and helps to encourage safe working practices. It can contribute positively to the health and safety culture, and is needed at all levels, including top management. Suitable induction arrangements need to be made for all recruits who are new to a site; this is particularly important for young recruits and those who are new to the industry.

* EPIC, the national training organisation for the extractive and mineral processing industries, has developed such standards, in collaboration with the industry and HSE, and can advise further on training (see Appendix 6 for address).

77   Induction needs to cover all matters which are site-specific. This includes relevant aspects of the health and safety policy statement, the health and safety document, risk assessments, the arrangements for first aid, fire, evacuation and blasting procedures. Further training is likely to be needed whenever:

(a)   someone takes on substantial new responsibilities; or

(b)   there is a significant change in work equipment or systems of work.

78   A person's competence will decline if skills are not used regularly. Training may, therefore, need to be repeated periodically to ensure continued competence in the skills that are not often used.

79   Information from personal performance, health and safety monitoring, accident investigation and near-miss incidents can help identify a need for additional training.

Instructions, rules and schemes

(1)   It shall be the duty of the operator to -

(a)   ensure that rules are in place at the quarry with a view to securing -

  (i)   the health and safety of those persons identified in regulation 7(1)(b)(i) and (ii), and

  (ii)   the safe use of equipment;

(b)   ensure that copies of all current instructions, rules and schemes required to be made under these Regulations are kept at the quarry and are -

  (i)   given to any person at work at the quarry upon whom they impose duties; and

  (ii)   comprehensible to all persons at work at the quarry to whom they apply; and

(c)   take all reasonable measures to ensure that each person at work at the quarry understands any rules required to be made under these Regulations which are relevant to that person.

(2)   The operator shall ensure, so far as is reasonably practicable, that any instructions, rules and schemes required to be made under these Regulations are followed, or as the case may be, complied with, by persons at work at the quarry.

80   The aim of the rules (operating procedures) required by these Regulations is to ensure the health and safety of the quarry workforce and others who may be at risk. Such rules have generally been known as the Manager's Rules. Regulation 10 requires the preparation of any rules needed for reasons of health and safety, for example those regarding the wearing of safety helmets, and the implementation of control measures based on assessment. Other regulations explicitly require written rules in relation to vehicles, shotfiring, excavations and tips.

81   All rules need to be given to and easily understood by those who have to enforce or follow them. They must also be clearly explained so that the people concerned understand them. All the rules must be reviewed in accordance with regulation 11.

Review of health and safety measures

The operator shall ensure that -

    (a)   the measures taken to protect the health and safety of those persons identified in regulation 7(1)(b)(i) and (ii) are reviewed -

        (i)   on a regular basis to ensure compliance with the relevant statutory provisions, and

        (ii) whenever the circumstances require it, including where there has been a significant change in the way that the quarry operates; and

    (b)   the regularity with which such reviews are to take place is specified in the health and safety document.

82   Health and safety measures need to be systematically and routinely monitored and reviewed* to ensure they are working as intended. They may fail because people are ignorant of them, are too busy to follow them or don't consider them to be important. They may also fail because the measures are out of date or flawed. Such failings will only become evident if the measures are reviewed and monitored. Action should then be taken to remedy any failings which have been identified, and to ensure that everyone follows the health and safety measures in future.

83   The arrangements for review need to address safety procedures and people's behaviour, as well as physical safeguards. This helps to identify procedures that have fallen into disrepute and to determine why. For example, a machinery guard which is regularly left off may indicate either a need to explain the risk, or to modify the guarding, system of work or supervision, to ensure that the safe way of working is also the easiest.

84   The findings from review need to be used to update and revise the health and safety measures. This feedback loop ensures continued effectiveness and contributes to a progressive improvement in health and safety.

85   Reviews are likely to be required when equipment or working practices change significantly, when new technology is introduced and after accidents, including 'near misses'. Such incidents provide opportunities to identify weaknesses and to change people's attitudes for the better. This opportunity should not be missed. But it is also important to identify the root causes of an incident in any investigation.

86   Learning from experience like this is known as reactive monitoring. Although this is very important, it is essential that there are also procedures for checking that systems and procedures are working without waiting until something goes wrong. This is known as active monitoring.

87   The operator should encourage those who work at the quarry to notify their manager, or some other designated person, of any shortcoming in the health and safety arrangements, even when no immediate danger exists. This provides valuable information which contributes to the review process.

---

* This process includes what is often known as auditing. Further information about this may be found in HSG65 *Successful health and safety management* (HSE Books 1997 ISBN 0 7176 1276 7).

Part III   Risk control

Inspection

(1)   The operator shall -

(a)   prepare and keep up to date a suitable written scheme for the systematic inspection, maintenance and, where appropriate, testing of -

(i)   all parts of the quarry,

(ii)   all buildings (whether temporary or permanent) at the quarry, and

(iii)   any plant at the quarry,

with a view to securing the health and safety of those persons identified in regulation 7(1)(b)(i) and (ii);

(b)   ensure that, where appropriate, suitable written reports are made of inspections, maintenance and tests carried out in pursuance of sub-paragraph (a) and that each report records significant defects and the steps taken to remedy them and -

(i)   is signed by the person making it, and

(ii)   countersigned by an appropriate person in the management structure; and

(c)   ensure that a sufficient number of competent persons are appointed to undertake the activities referred to in sub-paragraphs (a) and (b).

(2)   Without prejudice to the generality of paragraphs (1)(a) and (b), the said written scheme shall specify that faces above -

(a)   every place of work at the quarry; and

(b)   every road used by persons at work at the quarry for the purpose of their work or of getting to or from their place of work,

are inspected for loose ground or loose rocks before any work at the quarry commences or re-commences.

(3)   In this regulation, "inspection" means such visual or more rigorous inspection by a competent person as is appropriate for the purpose.

88   This section should be read in conjunction with requirements relating to inspection, examination and maintenance in other legislation and, in particular, the:

(a)   Provision and Use of Work Equipment Regulations 1998 (PUWER);[4]

(b)   Control of Substances Hazardous to Health Regulations 1999;[5]

(c)   Pressure Systems and Transportable Gas Containers Regulations 1989;[18]

(d)   Electricity at Work Regulations 1989;[19] and

(e)   Lifting Operations and Lifting Equipment Regulations 1998.[11]

89   This regulation requires a scheme for the inspection and maintenance of the whole quarry and its plant. This should take account of the inspection, maintenance and schemes for periodic thorough examination required under the regulations listed in paragraph 88; **it is not a substitute for them**. This regulation is, in relation to work equipment, a development of the duties of employers and the self-employed under regulations 6 and 22 of PUWER. Inspection and maintenance work carried out under other regulations does not need to be repeated.

90   Regulation 6(4) of PUWER requires work equipment being brought onto the site from another undertaking to be accompanied by evidence that it has been properly inspected. The scheme will be sufficient if these records are checked at appropriate intervals - as long as they are found to be satisfactory.

91   An inspection may vary from a simple visual inspection to a thorough examination, involving some dismantling and/or testing. The level of detail needs to be sufficient to ensure that no one is likely to be put at risk. Where a visual inspection is adequate for this purpose, dismantling or testing is not required.

92   The scheme needs to target those areas of the quarry and its plant which are liable to create significant risks* (including off-site risks) if conditions deteriorate. These areas should have been identified in the health and safety document as a result of risk assessments, and geotechnical appraisals or assessments.

93   The detail of the scheme for the quarry will also depend on the work activities, the nature of the materials, face and tip heights and weather conditions. For example, periods of heavy rain may result in loose materials, failures of tips and faces, and roads being washed away.

94   The scheme needs to include information on the frequency and level of detail of inspection, and the experience and any qualifications required by the people involved. It should, where necessary, include practical advice as to what defects are significant and on the action to be taken if defects are found, particularly in cases of imminent risk.

95   It is particularly important that the scheme covers:

(a)   vehicles;

(b)   machinery guarding;

(c)   safety devices such as reversing aids, interlocks and trip wires and emergency equipment required under regulation 15;

(d)   quarry electrical equipment;

(e)   pressure systems, including any air receivers on vehicles;

(f)   pedestrian routes, roadways and any edge protection;

(g)   excavations and tips;

* Regulation 6 of PUWER and its ACOP and guidance provide further information about significant risks and what needs to be inspected as far as work equipment is concerned. A risk will be significant if it could foreseeably result in death or serious personal injury, including adverse health effects.

(h)   buildings or other structures where a significant reduction in structural integrity, for example by corrosion, decay, overloading or impact damage, is forseeable; and

(i)   any barriers around the quarry required under regulation 16.

96   It is likely that the scheme will take the form of a general instruction, to which more detailed schedules for different types of plant and areas are attached.

97   Faces above working places or roads must be inspected before work starts to ensure that loose ground or rocks do not create significant risks. In other cases where the rate of deterioration or the risk is high, inspection will also be required at least once a shift. These inspections may identify a need for maintenance work, such as scaling, or influence its frequency.

98   In all cases, the frequency of inspection needs to be reviewed in the light of experience.

Imminent risks

99   If an imminent risk of serious personal injury is discovered during an inspection, the scheme must require immediate action to safeguard those at risk. This may include, for example, suspension of work in the area or taking an item of plant out of use.

100   Situations where such action is likely to be appropriate include:

(a)   loose ground or rocks above a roadway or workplace;

(b)   a vehicle with inefficient brakes or faulty steering;

(c)   missing edge protection on roads, benches, ramps and tipping points; and

(d)   machinery with missing guards or faulty safety devices.

Records of inspection and maintenance

101   Records* should be kept of all inspections, unless this would involve disproportionate effort, for example where small tools are inspected by the user before use and the time taken to carry out the inspection is less than the time to record it. Records will always be required, however, where significant defects are found, unless the tool is immediately scrapped. They are also required for any third-party periodic inspections carried out, for example by a storekeeper.

102   Records must show when the inspection was carried out, details of any significant defects found and remedial action taken. Significant defects are those which:

(a)   create a significant risk (see paragraph 92); or

(b)   may indicate the existence of a significant design or maintenance problem.

103   The report must be signed by the person making it, and countersigned by an appropriate manager or supervisor. This needs to be someone who can judge whether proposed remedial measures are

---

* These records may be computerised and signatures may be secure digital signatures which identify individuals.

appropriate and authorise them. Types of defect which need to be brought to the personal attention of the quarry manager, or other designated person, should be identified in the scheme.

104 Sometimes equipment is inspected by, or on behalf of, the operator, although it belongs to another person, for example a hire company or a contractor. In such cases, the owner should be informed of any defects found.

105 Anyone who notices a hazard related to the condition of the quarry or its equipment should bring it to the attention of a supervisor or manager.

Benches and haul roads

The operator shall ensure, so far as is reasonably practicable, that –

> *(a) benches and haul roads are designed, constructed and maintained so as to allow vehicles and plant to be used and moved upon them safely; and*

> *(b) where necessary, effective precautions are taken, by the installation of barriers or otherwise, to prevent vehicles or plant accidentally leaving any bench or haul road.*

106 The proper design of benches and haul roads is essential. They must be suitable for the type and size of machinery and loads used on them. Vehicles must be able to move safely and without risk of accidentally leaving the bench or from any instability of the face or bench. The operator also needs to consider the effect of vibration on the bench or haul road from any use of explosives.

107 The minimum width of the bench and the type of machinery which can be safely used on it should be considered during the design, appraisal and, where appropriate, the geotechnical assessment of the excavation or tip. They should be reviewed as the working methods and the excavation or tip develop. Benches need to be wide enough for the type and volume of traffic using them and take account of the traffic systems in force, for example one-way systems.

108 Benches and haul roads must be designed to avoid dangerous sharp bends and gradients. They must also be maintained so that they do not develop bumps, ruts or potholes which may make control of vehicles difficult or cause health problems due to whole-body vibration.

109 Regulation 17 of the Workplace (Health, Safety and Welfare) Regulations 1992 (the Workplace Regulations), which applies to quarries, deals with the organisation etc of traffic routes. Operators must take the regulation and relevant sections of the Approved Code of Practice into account when making arrangements to comply with regulation 13 of the Quarries Regulations. The design and construction of traffic routes inside buildings is also covered by regulation 12 of the Workplace Regulations.

Edge protection on roads

110 Adequate edge protection must be provided where there is a drop, lagoon or other hazard which would put the driver, or others, at significant risk if the vehicle left the bench or roadway. The aim of the edge protection is to stop the largest, fully loaded vehicle crossing it when travelling at the maximum foreseeable speed and it should be constructed with this in mind.

111   Edge protection may consist of purpose-made crash barriers or suitable bunds made from quarried material, for example scalpings.

112   On benches or roads used by heavy vehicles, the minimum acceptable height of the edge protection is 1.5 m or the radius of the largest wheel/tyre - whichever is greater. Additional protection is needed in high-risk areas, such as sharp bends or steep haul roads, where sand traps should also be considered.

113   Bunds can deteriorate due to weathering, and so must be properly inspected in accordance with the scheme required under regulation 12. Where necessary to ensure the drainage of surface water, gaps may be left in the bunds, or other drainage systems provided. Any gaps must not be wide enough for a vehicle to pass through.

114   Edge protection less than either 1.5 m, or the radius of the vehicle wheel, or with sloping sides, makes an ideal ramp for the vehicle to run over, and is totally ineffective (see Figure 1).

115   Blocks of stone placed along the edge of a bench, ramp or roadway which can be easily pushed out of the way by a vehicle are not suitable for edge protection (see Figure 2).

116   A bank of unconsolidated material like scalpings is suitable if it is big enough to allow the vehicle's momentum to be absorbed. The impact face needs to be as nearly vertical as possible and the height as described in paragraph 112 (see Figure 3).

117   Rocks can be used if they can safely absorb the impact, for example by heaping materials like scalpings between and behind the rocks to provide an adequate barrier. A violent stop due to impact with large rocks would, of course, increase the risk of injury to the driver, and of damage to the vehicle, and so should be avoided (see Figure 4).

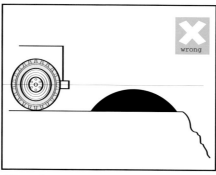

Figure 1

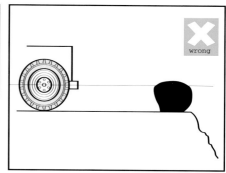

Figure 2

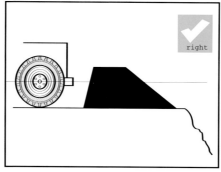

Figure 3

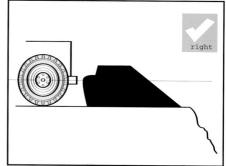

Figure 4

Rules controlling risk from vehicles

The operator shall make suitable and sufficient rules (known in these Regulations as the "vehicles rules") which shall lay down in writing measures designed to control the risks to persons at the quarry arising from the use of vehicles at the quarry.

118 Thirteen people were killed in transport-related accidents at quarries between 1993 and 1998, and about 60 were seriously injured. Three quarry workers were killed and 12 seriously injured by reversing or moving vehicles. These types of accidents accounted for over 60% of the fatal accidents at quarries. It is therefore vitally important that the hazards associated with vehicles are identified and the risks controlled. Good, well-enforced, vehicles rules can make a significant contribution to reducing deaths and injuries.

119 These rules are wider in scope than those provided under previous legislation. Rules must now deal with the safe management of all vehicles and mobile machinery on site; rules which cover only instructions for drivers are not sufficient. The rules must cover contractors' and private vehicles, as well as railway trains on private railways or sidings within the quarry.

120 These rules may form part of the general rules required by regulation 10, and should be brought to the attention of those affected and reviewed as required in regulation 11.

121 There is considerable overlap between the requirements of this regulation, PUWER and the Workplace Regulations. However, vehicles rules are included in these Regulations because of the special considerations which apply in quarries and the record of the industry in relation to vehicle safety. Appendix 4 includes general guidance on vehicle safety in quarries under PUWER and the Workplace Regulations.

122 These rules need to be set out in a way which takes account of how risks vary from one part of the quarry to another. For example, rules for the excavation area might be irrelevant elsewhere and some vehicles may be banned from certain areas.

123 In particular, the rules need to cover:

(a) how drivers are to be assessed for competence and authorised to operate vehicles (PUWER regulation 9, paragraph 194);

(b) security arrangements, including control of keys (PUWER regulation 28, paragraph 364);

(c) any restrictions on where vehicles may be used, for example due to height, width, gradient (Workplace Regulations, regulation 17, paragraph 163);

(d) any restrictions on reversing (Workplace Regulations, regulation 17, paragraph 167);

(e) speed limits (Workplace Regulations, regulation 17, paragraph 164);

(f) restrictions on traffic routes, for example one-way arrangements (Workplace Regulations, regulation 17, paragraphs 163-167);

(g) pedestrian safety (Workplace Regulations, regulation 17, paragraphs 171 and 175 and PUWER paragraph 45);

(h) fitting and use of safety devices, including seat belts and visibility aids (PUWER regulations 17, 26, 28, paragraphs 352, 369, 370);

(i)   use of vehicles in adverse conditions, for example fog, rain, ice, mud etc;

(j)   precautions where quarry vehicles or trailers with tipping bodies or tipping gear are loaded, unloaded or sheeted (Workplace Regulations, regulation 13, paragraphs 138-140);

(k)   instructions to drivers concerning the reporting of defects; and

(l)   relevant cross-references to the scheme for inspection and maintenance of plant.

Note: The paragraph references in (a) to (j) refer to the relevant ACOP guidance.

Escape and rescue facilities at the quarry

The operator shall ensure that -

(a)   adequate means of escape and rescue are provided and maintained so as to permit persons in the quarry to leave the quarry promptly and safely in the event of danger;

(b)   adequate means of communication and warning are provided to enable assistance, escape and rescue operations to be launched at once when required;

(c)   written instructions concerning the use of emergency equipment and the action to be taken in the event of an emergency at or near the quarry are prepared;

(d)   persons at work at the quarry are trained in appropriate action to be taken in the event of an emergency; and

(e)   rescue equipment is provided at readily accessible, appropriately sited and clearly sign-posted places and kept ready for use.

124 This regulation requires the operator to ensure the provision of adequate means of escape and rescue in the event of danger. Risk assessments should indicate the emergencies which might arise and the action and equipment required to deal with them.

125 Particular attention should be paid to means of escape from areas such as rooms, chambers, confined spaces* and other areas where there is a significant risk from:

(a)   fire;

(b)   the escape of steam;

(c)   concentration of noxious gases; or

(d)   ground collapse, for example in stockpile tunnels or other rock cavities or tunnels to which people have access in the course of their work.

126 Means of escape need to be taken into account when designing both fixed and mobile workplaces. Sometimes a second exit may be necessary, for example in some areas where highly flammable liquids are used.

* The Confined Spaces Regulations 1997 may also apply.

Communications

127 Good communications are of paramount importance in an emergency, particularly in remote areas and for lone workers. Suitable communication equipment might range from bells to more sophisticated public address or closed-circuit television systems. Radios or telephones* can enable rapid communication, if they are carefully positioned. They may, for example, be fitted to mobile plant or backup service vehicles, or issued to appropriate individuals.

128 In most quarries, liaison with the emergency services is helpful. In particular, it is advisable to inform them in advance of any dangers that might affect their operations, for example the presence of explosives, LPG (liquefied petroleum gas) storage, unstable faces and burning tyres which may explode.

129 Well-constructed and maintained roadways allow emergency vehicles easier access. These vehicles are generally made for road use, and are not suited to difficult terrain. In an emergency it can be helpful to have a person waiting at the quarry entrance to direct the emergency services.

Rescue equipment

130 Examples of the type of rescue equipment which may be required include:

(a)   breathing apparatus (see also regulation 21(2));

(b)   ropes;

(c)   ladders (rigid or rope);

(d)   tripods, winches;

(e)   tools, eg pickaxe, crowbar, shovel, cutters;

(f)   stretchers;

(g)   buoyancy aids, eg lifejackets, lifebuoys (rings); and

(h)   rescue boats.

131 Lifting and cutting equipment may also be needed in some quarries. Emergency equipment must be subject to appropriate inspection, as required by regulation 12, to ensure that it is always ready for use.

Training

132 Most people only need to be able to leave their workplace and go to a designated place of safety in the event of an emergency. Where rescue equipment is provided, enough people should be trained to use it without endangering themselves or others. If breathing apparatus is required, there must be enough trained people to use it safely.

133 Regulation 3(2) of the Health and Safety (First Aid) Regulations 1981[20] requires an employer to ensure the provision of enough trained personnel to administer first aid.

---

* Electrical systems, radios or mobile telephones may be unsuitable where explosives are in use or where there is a risk of an explosive atmosphere and the equipment may cause ignition or initiate the explosion.

Barriers

The operator shall ensure that, where appropriate, a barrier suitable for the purpose of discouraging trespass is placed around the boundary of the quarry and is properly maintained.

134 Employers and the self-employed have a general duty, under section 3 of the HSW Act, to ensure, so far as is reasonably practicable, the safety of those not in their employment. This regulation goes further by specifically requiring, where appropriate, the provision and maintenance of suitable barriers around the quarry to discourage trespass. In this context, trespass means entry to the quarry without the operator's express or implied permission or some legal justification.

135 Barriers are appropriate where it is reasonably foreseeable that members of the public, including children, are likely to trespass on the site and could suffer injury if they did so. There is a significant risk of injury to trespassers at most quarries. Barriers should always be provided at quarry boundaries which are near to schools, colleges, shops or significant numbers of homes.

136 The provision of barriers needs to be considered as part of the risk assessment process, and the findings of the assessment included in the health and safety document. Any decision not to provide barriers for any part of the quarry needs to be reviewed in the light of experience. In particular, the adequacy of the arrangements should be carefully reconsidered if there is evidence of children playing on, or near, the site.

137 The type of barrier required depends on the risks. In a rural area where the risk of public access is low, hedges, trenches and mounds may be enough. At the other extreme, where there is evidence of persistent trespass by children which places them at significant risk, sophisticated metal paling fences may be required.*

138 Everyone should be encouraged to report cases of trespass or evidence that children have been playing on the site. They should also be told what action to take if they discover trespassers.

139 Records must be kept to show that barriers have been appropriately inspected and repaired in accordance with the scheme set up under regulation 12.

140 Section 151 of the Mines and Quarries Act 1954, which is enforced by local authorities, requires working and abandoned quarries to be provided with a barrier to prevent anyone accidentally falling into the quarry. Barriers must also be provided where the quarry constitutes a danger to members of the public.

141 Section 151 enables the local authority to take steps to enforce the provision of barriers if the quarry is considered to be a statutory nuisance under the Environmental Protection Act 1990. It remains in force alongside these Regulations.

* The Health and Safety Commission publication *Prevention of trespass and vandalism on railways* (ISBN 0 7176 1661 4) contains some interesting case studies regarding the way that problems with trespass have been addressed. It may be useful for quarries experiencing particular problems.

Regulation 17

Compliance with Part IV

Regulation

17

The operator shall ensure that regulations 18 to 23 are in each case complied with as appropriate having regard to the features of the quarry, the nature and circumstances of the work carried on there or to a specific risk.

Guidance

17

142 This regulation provides operators some flexibility in the implementation of regulations 18 to 23. Its purpose is to ensure that any action required is in proportion to the actual hazards and risks. It allows operators to take account of the features of the quarry and the work carried on there when deciding what, if any, action needs to be taken in relation to these Regulations.

Regulation 18

Permits to work

Regulation

18

(1) The operator shall ensure that a system is in place so as to ensure that any work involving -

(a) the carrying out of hazardous operations; or

(b) usually straightforward operations which may interact with other activities to cause serious hazards,

is not carried out unless a permit to carry out that work has been issued.

(2) Such permits to work shall specify -

(a) the conditions to be fulfilled; and

(b) the precautions to be taken before, during and after the operation concerned,

in order to ensure, so far as is reasonably practicable, the health and safety of any person affected by that operation.

(3) Such permits to work shall be -

(a) issued, signed and dated by a suitable person in the management structure; and then

(b) accepted, signed and dated by a further suitable person.

Guidance

18

What is a permit to work?

143 A safe system of work is required* for all work activities. A permit-to-work system[21,22] is a formal procedure to ensure that the system of work is properly planned and implemented for jobs which are potentially highly dangerous. Permits are most often required for maintenance work where normal safeguards cannot be used, or when new hazards are introduced by the work. They should not generally be used for low-risk operations, as this tends to devalue the system.

144 A permit to work should not be confused with giving someone permission to work on a site; nor is it an excuse to carry out a dangerous job without eliminating hazards or minimising risks.

* HSW Act section 2.

31

145 Issuing a permit does not, by itself, make a job safe. That can be achieved only by the diligence of those preparing, supervising and carrying out the work. The system does, however, provide a formal procedure to determine, systematically, what precautions are required, how this should be communicated, recorded and monitored, and how work should be authorised.

146 In some straightforward high-hazard situations, simple systems of work such as isolation or locking-off procedures are sufficient, by themselves, to ensure safety. Regulation 19 of the Provision and Use of Work Equipment Regulations 1998 and the guidance to that provides more information about isolation procedures. Such systems are generally appropriate when there is only a single source of danger which can be eliminated by, for example, removing a fuse and locking off an electrical isolator switch. In more complicated cases, for example where there are several sources of danger, or where complex procedures are needed before it is safe to start work, a permit to work is usually appropriate.

147 The aim of a permit-to-work system is to ensure that the task is carried out in accordance with the carefully considered conditions specified in a permit drawn up and independently verified by competent individuals.

148 As well as setting out the steps which must be taken before and during a job, permits should state any conditions to be met after the work is completed, ie the procedure for handing back the plant or area for normal operational use.

149 A permit-to-work system forms an essential element in the safety management system of the quarry. Risk assessments under regulation 3 of the Management of Health and Safety at Work Regulations 1999 will help the operator to identify circumstances where permits to work are needed.

The permit-to-work system

150 Permits to work are required whenever there is a significant risk* of death or serious injury during an operation, and where precise preparation of the site or plant and clear, unambiguous communication of procedures is needed to control this risk.

151 A permit-to-work system should set out:

(a) what work requires permits;

(b) who is authorised to issue and accept permits, including any limitations to their authority;

(c) how the safety of a proposed system of work and any risks it might create for others is checked - this may include cross-referencing with any other relevant permits;

(d) how information about the hazards and the work to be carried out is communicated;

(e) the maximum time a permit may be valid;

(f) hand-over arrangements if work involves more than one team, eg over a shift change;

* This includes risks to health.

(g)   the handback/suspension arrangements in cases where:

  (i)   the permit is found to be flawed or unsuitable - for example because assumptions on which it was based are incorrect;

  (ii)   more time is needed to carry out the work than the permit allows;

(h)   arrangements for the display of the permit at the work site;

(i)   arrangements for hand-over on completion of the work; and

(j)   arrangements for monitoring and revising the system and its operation.

152   Examples of work at a quarry likely to require a permit include:

(a)   entry into confined spaces[10] or other danger areas designated under regulation 22;

(b)   entry into machinery (eg mixers) where isolation or locking-off procedures are insufficient (see paragraph 146) to ensure the safety of workers; and

(c)   work on complicated or high-voltage electrical systems.

Issuing a permit

153   Two people are responsible for each permit: the person issuing the permit (normally the manager responsible for the plant or location where the work is to be performed) and the person accepting it (normally the supervisor for the work to be done). These two people should independently consider the risks and precautions, as this substantially reduces the chance of overlooking important issues.

154   Expert advice may also be required to determine the hazards and to decide what precautions are required, for example atmospheric testing. Such experts must have sufficient experience and knowledge to carry out their tasks properly.

Communication and training

155   All staff involved with permits to work need to understand both the system and their own role. This is particularly important in relation to the people issuing and accepting permits.

156   In addition, everybody involved must understand the hazards and the precautions for each individual job. This cannot be achieved by simply giving everyone a copy of the permit. There needs to be appropriate formal briefing to ensure that everyone understands exactly what is required and why. The use of plans or diagrams may help with some work. Those involved also need to know when work covered by the permit may begin and whether there are any time or other constraints.

157   There should be formal hand-over arrangements if more than one team is involved with the work, for example at a shift change.

Monitoring

158   Suitable arrangements for monitoring the operation of the permit-to-work system are essential. They typically involve testing a sample of permits to ensure that they are completed correctly, and that the precautions are

appropriate and followed in practice.

Safety drills

(1)   The operator shall ensure that safety drills are held at regular intervals for persons at work at the quarry.

(2)   Such safety drills shall be for the following purposes -

(a)   to train the persons who work at the quarry in the appropriate actions to be taken in an emergency including, where appropriate, the correct use, handling or operation of emergency equipment; and

(b)   to train and check the skills of such persons to whom specific duties involving the use, handling or operation of such equipment have been assigned in the event of an emergency.

159   The risk assessments should identify the type of emergencies which may occur and consequently the safety drills which will be of value. The people involved in such drills, the areas covered and the number of drills that are needed should be decided based on these assessments, and also by taking account of regulation 15.

160   Safety drills help ensure that people know what to do in an emergency. In particular, they help those likely to be involved in escape and rescue operations familiarise themselves with procedures and equipment. In some situations it may be useful to carry out safety drills in conjunction with the emergency services.

Fire and explosion hazards

(1)   The operator shall ensure that no person at work at the quarry uses a naked flame or carries out any work which could give rise to a risk of an unintended explosion or fire unless sufficient measures to prevent such an explosion or fire are taken.

(2)   No person shall smoke in any part of a quarry where there is a risk of fire or explosion.

161   Hot work should not be permitted near closed vessels which contain, or have contained flammable* substances, except under a permit-to-work system as described at regulation 18. Even a trace may create enough flammable vapour to cause a substantial explosion.

162   Hot work also needs to be prohibited on closed pressurised systems which could explode or fail as a result of heat. This includes tyres and wheels, which are often contaminated with grease or oil and create hazards from both pressure and flammable substances.

163   This regulation does not prohibit the use of a brazier or other open fire in properly controlled conditions.

* Flammable, in this context, includes substances which have flashpoints of over 55°C, but will burn or decompose at the temperatures involved in work such as welding and flame-cutting.

Control of harmful and explosive atmospheres

(1)   It shall be the duty of the operator to ensure that -

(a)   steps are taken in order to determine whether potentially explosive substances are present in the atmosphere and, where such substances are present, to measure the concentration of such substances in the atmosphere;

(b)   automatic devices designed to -

(i)   monitor continuously the concentration of explosive or flammable gases in the atmosphere,

(ii)   trigger an alarm if such concentration reaches a dangerous level, and

(iii)   cut off power to any plant which, because of the concentration of such gases in the atmosphere, gives rise to a risk to the health and safety of any person,

are provided;

(c)   where devices are provided in accordance with paragraph (b)(i), a record of the levels of concentration of such gases in the atmosphere shall be made at such intervals as are specified in the health and safety document;

(d)   at any place in the quarry where there is a risk of the occurrence or accumulation of an explosive atmosphere, all necessary measures are taken with a view to -

(i)   preventing such occurrence and accumulation, or, where this is not practicable,

(ii)   preventing the ignition of such an atmosphere; and

(e)   at any place in the quarry where there is a risk of the occurrence or accumulation of a substance harmful to health in the atmosphere, appropriate measures are taken in order to -

(i)   prevent such occurrence and accumulation, or, where this is not practicable,

(ii)   extract or disperse that harmful substance,

in such a way that persons are not placed at risk.

(2)   Without prejudice to the requirements of the Personal Protective Equipment Regulations 1992,[a] the operator shall ensure that whenever persons at work are present at any place in the quarry where they may be exposed to a substance harmful to health in the atmosphere -

(a)   appropriate and sufficient breathing and resuscitation equipment is available; and

(b)   a sufficient number of persons trained in the use of such equipment is present.

(3)   The operator shall ensure that the equipment referred to at paragraph (2)(a) is suitably stored and maintained.

21

(a) SI 1992/3139; amended by SI 1993/3074, 1994/2326, 1996/3039.

164 Work in most quarries is not likely to create a significant risk of an accumulation of explosive or flammable gases. If the risk is negligible then no action need be taken to comply with regulation 21(1) because of the way it is qualified by regulation 17. There are circumstances, however, in which such a risk could arise, for example as a result of methane from a neighbouring waste disposal site, or in a confined space.

165 Any possibility of significant concentrations of flammable gases on a site needs to be carefully assessed, and measurements taken to determine typical concentrations. The action required to comply with this regulation and to prevent explosions needs to be determined and recorded in the health and safety document.

166 Where flammable gases are likely to be found at above 25% of their lower explosive limit, the precautions listed in regulation 21(1)(b) need to be specified in the health and safety document.

167 It is strongly recommended that alarms, where fitted, are triggered as soon as the concentration of flammable gas exceeds 25% of its lower explosive limit.

168 Electrical* and any other equipment which is liable to be exposed to flammable vapours must be suitable for use in such conditions.

169 Power cut-off devices are not an alternative to using equipment designed for use in a flammable atmosphere. They are only appropriate where the risk of exposure to flammable vapours is low, and the act of cutting off the power would not itself create a risk of ignition, for example from an electrical spark.

170 Complying with the requirements of the Control of Substances Hazardous to Health Regulations 1999 (COSHH) will ensure compliance with regulation 21(1)(e), insofar as that regulation relates to the risk of exposure to substances hazardous to health as defined by COSHH.

* Regulation 6 of the Electricity at Work Regulations 1989.

Regulation 22

Danger areas

The operator shall ensure that -

    (a) any danger areas in the quarry are clearly marked;

    (b) equipment or barriers designed to prevent inadvertent entry by any unauthorised person are installed at any danger area in the quarry in which, because of the nature of the work being carried out there or for any other reason there is -

        (i) risk of a person falling a distance likely to cause personal injury,

        (ii) risk of a person being struck by a falling object likely to cause personal injury, or

        (iii) a significant risk to the health and safety of persons; and

    (c) where any person at work is authorised to enter a danger area, appropriate measures are taken to protect his health and safety.

171 The whole quarry is potentially dangerous, but there is nothing to be gained by treating it all as a danger area. This would simply devalue the term. Risk assessment should be used to identify those areas which merit being treated as a danger area.

172 Unauthorised people must be excluded from such areas, for example by placing warning signs and barriers around them. Workers should only be allowed to enter a danger area if it is essential and when appropriate

safeguards have been adopted. A safe system of work is always required, and this may involve a permit to work as explained at regulation 18.

173 Areas of the quarry where there are significant health hazards may need to be marked as danger areas, for example where there are high noise or dust levels. It is always better, however, to control these risks at source.

174 Areas of the quarry where access is forseeable and the risk is high should be treated as danger areas. Particular consideration needs to be given to:

(a)   sections of the excavation, particularly where there are significant overhangs, which are liable to collapse onto people;

(b)   edges of excavations, particularly water-filled excavations, which may collapse under the weight of people or equipment;

(c)   places from which people can fall more than 2 m or where falling a lesser distance could be particularly dangerous;

(d)   places where people are liable to be struck by falling objects such as stone falling from faces; or

(e)   places where there are materials which behave like quicksand and could drown people.

Barriers

175   No barrier can totally prevent access by a determined person, but barriers must:

(a)   clearly identify the boundary of the danger area; and

(b)   make entry impossible without a conscious effort.

176   Regulation 13 of the Workplace Regulations contains requirements regarding the prevention of falls and falling objects. The minimum standard for such barriers is 1100 mm high with a mid-rail, and usually a solid section at the bottom. Tensioned ropes or straps and earth bunds which provide equivalent protection are also acceptable.

Lighting

The operator shall ensure that every part of a quarry in which a person is likely to be exposed to risks in the event of the failure of artificial lighting is provided with emergency lighting of adequate intensity and where that is impractical persons at work in that place shall be provided with a personal lamp.

177   General lighting matters and emergency lighting inside buildings are covered by regulation 8 of the Workplace Regulations. Relevant advice is contained in the Approved Code of Practice to that regulation. Lighting a quarry is much more difficult than lighting a flat area because of the uneven surfaces and the consequential deceptive effects of shadows.

178 Emergency lighting is required where work continues after dark and safe evacuation is not possible without artificial lighting. Where lighting is provided by independently powered lighting towers and failure of any one tower would still leave enough light to enable people to leave the area safely, no further emergency lighting need be provided.

179 Lights provided on vehicles ought to be sufficient to enable them to be driven safely, but additional lighting may be required for manoeuvring operations such as reversing or tipping.

180 The safety of security staff and others who have to move around the quarry at night must be ensured by an appropriate combination of torches and floodlights.

Application of this Part

This Part shall apply to the storage, transport and use of explosives at a quarry.

181 The definition of explosives in regulation 2 refers to the definition of explosive articles and substances in the Classification and Labelling of Explosives Regulations 1983. In most cases it ought to be clear from a product's label if it is an explosive.

182 Under the 1983 Regulations:

(a) explosive substance means:

'any solid or liquid substance or any mixture of solid or liquid substances or both which is capable by chemical reaction in itself of producing gas at such a temperature and pressure and at such a speed as could cause damage to surroundings or which is designed to produce an effect by heat, light, sound, gas or smoke or a combination of these as a result of non-detonative self-sustaining exothermic chemical reactions.'

(b) explosive article means:

'any article containing any explosive substance or mixture'.

183 Detonators are an explosive article and so are explosives for the purposes of these Regulations.

184 Legislation which may apply to explosives in quarries in addition to these Regulations includes:

(a) Explosives Act 1875 (this is gradually being replaced by more modern legislation);

(b) Ammonium Nitrate Mixtures Exemption Order 1967;

(c) Control of Explosives Regulations 1991[23] (COER is mainly concerned with security and is enforced, in most cases, by the police);

(d) Placing on the Market and Supervision of Transfer of Explosives Regulations 1993 (these cover product safety and security during transfer);

(e) Packaging of Explosives for Carriage Regulations 1991;

(f) *Carriage of Dangerous Goods by Rail Regulations 1996;[24,25]

(g) *Carriage of Explosives by Road Regulations 1996; [25,26] and

(h) Transport of Dangerous Goods (Safety Advisers) Regulations 1999.

* The Regulations in items (f) and (g) were amended by the Carriage of Dangerous Goods (Amendment) Regulations 1999, SI 1999/303 which came into force on 5 March 1999.

Operator's duties

(1)   The operator shall -

(a)   ensure, so far as is reasonably practicable, that all explosives are stored, transported and used safely and securely;

(b)   appoint one or more competent individuals to organise and supervise all work at the quarry involving the use of explosives ("the Explosives Supervisor"); and

(c)   ensure that at no time is there more than one person acting as the Explosives Supervisor at the quarry.

(2)   It shall be the duty of the operator to ensure that -

(a)   suitable and sufficient rules are made which lay down in writing procedures for -

   (i)   shotfiring operations at the quarry,

   (ii)   appointing shotfirers, trainee shotfirers and storekeepers,

   (iii)   authorising other persons who will be involved with the storage, transport or use of explosives,

   (iv)   dealing with misfires, and

   (v)   ensuring, so far as is reasonably practicable, that such rules are complied with;

(b)   an adequate written specification (whether produced by him or not) is prepared for each shotfiring operation at the quarry to ensure, so far as is reasonably practicable, that when such firing occurs it will not give rise to danger; and

(c)   a copy of the specification referred to in sub-paragraph (b) is given to any person upon whom it imposes duties.

(3)   The operator shall ensure that operations involving the storage, transport or use of explosives are carried out by -

(a)   a duly authorised and competent person; or

(b)   a trainee under the close supervision of a duly authorised and competent person.

(4)   The operator shall ensure that -

(a)   such facilities and equipment as are necessary to enable shotfiring operations to be carried out safely are provided;

(b)   any vehicle which is provided for use in relation to shotfiring operations is so marked as to be readily identifiable from a distance;

(c)   detonators are stored in separate containers from other explosives; and

(d)   explosives are kept at all times either in a locked explosives store or under the constant supervision of a suitable person.

40

(5) The operator shall ensure, so far as is reasonably practicable, that each shotfiring operation is carried out safely and in accordance with the rules required to be made in pursuance of paragraph (2)(a) and any specification required to be prepared in pursuance of paragraph (2)(b).

185 The operator's key responsibility regarding the use of explosives, as in relation to other risks, is to ensure that the work is properly managed, planned, co-ordinated and supervised. The duties placed on the operator under this regulation reflect this. This is the case whether shotfiring operations are undertaken by a quarry worker or by a specialist blasting contractor.

Explosives supervisors

186 The explosives supervisor is the person in overall, day-to-day, charge of work with explosives at a quarry. Exactly who is appointed as an explosives supervisor will vary. It may, for example, be the quarry manager, another manager or supervisor, a blasting contractor, one of the contractor's employees or an outside consultant.

187 The operator must be satisfied that an explosives supervisor has sufficient practical and theoretical knowledge and experience for the work he/she is expected to do. To obtain the necessary theoretical knowledge, an explosives supervisor needs, as a minimum, to have successfully completed a course of training covering:

(a) blast calculation and design;

(b) ground vibration and air blast overpressure; and

(c) shotfiring (see Appendix 1).

188 A quarry may need several explosives supervisors to cover all the work, for example where blasting takes place on several shifts. If this is necessary for the working of the quarry:

(a) only one person may act as the explosives supervisor at any one time;

(b) all explosives supervisors must be familiar with the shotfiring rules and the site, as far as that relates to the safe use of explosives; and

(c) there needs to be good communication and co-ordination between them, for example to deal with any hand-over or maintenance issues.

Blasting contractors

189 The operator may appoint a contractor, the blasting contractor, to carry out some or all of the explosives work. The operator is, nevertheless, always responsible for the overall management of the quarry and safe use and security of explosives. The operator is similarly responsible for the shotfiring rules and blast specifications, even if a contractor or consultant actually draws them up.

190 Although the legal duties relating to explosives are placed on the operator, the blasting contractor may also be legally liable in some cases (see paragraph 45).

Shotfiring rules

191 The shotfiring rules are the practical operating procedures which are in place to ensure that shotfiring operations at the quarry take place without endangering the workforce or the public.

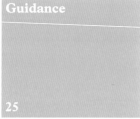

Guidance

25

ACOP

192 The rules need to take proper account of local circumstances, for example any risk of accidental initiation due to radio frequency transmitters, electrically powered plant and overhead power lines. If there is such a risk, a suitable method of initiation must be chosen.

193 They need to be well-publicised throughout the quarry, and personal copies given to those who have duties under them. The operator must ensure that arrangements are made to monitor compliance with the rules.

194 The rules need to cover arrangements for:

(a) the appointment and authorisation of shotfirers, trainee shotfirers, storekeepers and others working with explosives;

(b) the explosives supervisor to check that:

(i) the equipment provided is suitable and safe; and

(ii) site conditions are in line with the blast specification before work with explosives;

(c) times when shotfiring is permitted;*

(d) the determination of the danger zone† likely to be created by the firing of each shot, evacuation of the danger zone and the provision of effective shelters when a shot is tested or fired;

(e) warning systems including, as appropriate:

(i) the use of flags or notices;

(ii) a system of audible signals** to warn people to withdraw from the danger zone and to give the all-clear;

(iii) the posting of sentries before each shot; and

(iv) the direct personal notification of local residents who may be affected;

(f) inspection of the blast site after firing to check the state of the face and whether a misfire has occurred;

(g) ensuring that normal working is resumed only when the shotfirer is fully satisfied that it is safe and the all-clear has been sounded;

(h) safeguarding charged, but unfired,‡ shotholes at the end of a working day. These arrangements should ensure that someone is in attendance, or within sight of the charged holes, to prevent theft or unauthorised initiation of the explosives (including detonators);

(i) dealing with misfires and the discovery of unfired explosives from previous operations. There must always be a competent person available,*** normally the explosives supervisor, to ensure that any misfire is dealt with safely; and

* See regulation 29(4)(a). These times should also be posted where anyone that might be affected can see them.
† The danger zone does not include any safe refuge, for example one from which a shot is to be fired, which is deliberately excluded from what would otherwise be the danger zone.
** The signals must be audible throughout the danger zone.
‡ This includes explosives left after a misfire which have not been recovered by the end of the working day.
*** This does not mean that there must always be an explosives supervisor on site, but there should always be someone of that level of competence who can be contacted to advise how to deal with a misfire and, if necessary, to take personal charge.

25

(j) monitoring arrangements for operations to ensure the rules are complied with.

Blasting specification

195 The purpose of the blasting specification is to prevent danger during the firing of shots. The blasting specification must be tailored for each blast, in view of the conditions on the site.

196 The specification should be designed to:

(a) ensure that the risk of flyrock being projected outside the declared danger zone is as low as reasonably practicable, and should state any special precautions required to achieve this;

(b) minimise the risk of misfires;

(c) enable the location of any misfired shots to be determined accurately; and

(d) ensure that faces are left in a safe condition after a blast.

197 The specification should take account of:

(a) experience gained from previous blasts at the quarry;

(b) any unusual circumstances which are present or likely to arise; and

(c) the design of the excavation.

198 Appendix 2 lists matters to be considered when preparing for a blast and details which need to be recorded.

Security of explosives

199 The arrangements and responsibilities for the storage and security of explosives on site must minimise the risk of loss or theft. Requirements regarding the security of explosives at a particular site may be set out in the store's explosives licence.[27] If necessary, advice should be obtained from the licensing authority and/or the police.

200 Only authorised people may handle explosives at a quarry (see regulation 29(1)). In addition, employers must not knowingly employ a 'prohibited person' as defined in regulation 2(1) of the Control of Explosives Regulations 1991 in a position where they handle or have control of any explosive or any restricted substance.

201 The keys to the explosives store must be kept safe at all times, either in the custody of the explosives supervisor, shotfirer or explosives storekeeper, or in a secure place.

202 To ensure the safety and security of the explosives there should be appropriate arrangements for authorising all movements of explosives to and from the place of use. Authorisation is usually by the explosives supervisor.

203 The duties of the storekeeper in charge of the explosives store include:

(a) the security and safe storage of explosives, including detonators;

(b)   the custody of keys;

(c)   record-keeping;

(d)   the issue and receipt of explosives; and

(e)   immediately reporting any loss or theft of explosives to a designated person.

Custody of explosives etc

204 Explosives must be issued only to an authorised person, such as a shotfirer or trainee shotfirer. They must remain under the control of such a person.

205 Containers for detonators must be fitted with secure locks. Electrically operated detonators must be stored so that they are electrically isolated, with no part of any detonator or lead exposed. The container must be lined with shock-absorbing, antistatic material, kept clean and used only for detonators. Containers should be unlocked for as short a time as possible - only while detonators are actually being inserted or removed.

206 Other explosives must be carried in the manufacturer's packaging or other suitable, robust containers, and removed from the packaging or container only immediately before use.

207 Ammonium nitrate needs to be kept in weatherproof and well-ventilated conditions. It must be protected from contamination by fuel oil or other organic material. This can usually be achieved by keeping it 25 m away from any stored explosives, fuel or lubricating oil. To minimise the risk of fire, the surrounding area needs to be kept clear of grass, shrubbery, spilled fuel oil, or other organic material.

208 Where deliveries of explosives (including detonators) are made directly to the blast site, the shotfirer needs to check the delivery note to ensure that the quantities are correct, sign for them and ensure they are not left unattended. The detonators must be transferred to suitably constructed detonator containers as soon as possible. To enable accurate record-keeping, the delivery note needs to be passed to the person in charge of the explosives store.

Disposal of empty cases and deteriorated explosives

209 There should be arrangements to check that no explosive remains hidden or lodged within any explosives cases before disposal. Manufacturers can advise on the removal or destruction of deteriorated explosives.[28]

Use of vehicles to transport explosives etc

210 Parts of vehicles where explosives are carried must be kept clean and free of grit. Detonators must be kept in appropriate containers and enclosed in a strong, locked compartment when they are being carried on a vehicle. Explosives must be loaded safely, so that they cannot fall out of the vehicle.

211 Nothing which creates a fire or detonation risk must be carried on a vehicle containing explosives or ammonium nitrate. Anything else which is carried must be safely stored, normally in suitable separate compartments or containers. It is good practice to ensure that only essential shotfiring equipment (circuit-testers, stemming rods and shotfiring cable) is carried on such vehicles.

212 All vehicles transporting explosives (including detonators) in the quarry must be provided with enough, suitable fire extinguishers. They must also be easily recognisable from a distance, for example by means of signs, distinctive flashing lights or flags.

213 Trailers must have efficient brakes and a properly designed rigid tow bar with a safety chain, which will cause the brake to be applied in the event of separation.

Provision and maintenance of equipment

214 The equipment provided for shotfiring operations must be suitable and properly maintained. Inspection and maintenance arrangements must be set out in the scheme required under regulation 12. Regulations 4, 5, 6 and 7 of PUWER are also relevant.

215 The explosives supervisor should check that the equipment provided is suitable and safe. Any equipment the explosives supervisor does not believe is safe should be taken out of use.

Shotfiring equipment

216 Circuit-testers must be capable of measuring the resistance of the circuit without any adverse effect on the detonators. Where transformer coupled electric detonators are used, an impedance test facility is required. This often forms an integral part of the exploder.

217 Exploders and circuit-testers need detailed inspection, including appropriate tests, at periods specified by the manufacturer or every six months, whichever is shorter. Such inspection is also needed after any significant repair or an unexplained misfire.

218 The inspections and tests should be designed to ensure that exploders and circuit-testers are in good order and meet their designed performance ratings and that exploders can fire shots up to their rated capacities. A record of the results of any inspections and tests must be retained for a period of three years (see regulation 44).

219 Tools used for piercing cartridges, mixing explosives or in shotholes (eg for charging, stemming or testing) must be made of non-sparking materials such as wood, antistatic plastic or non-ferrous metal.

220 Electric detonators must not be used inside shotholes where there is a risk of premature detonation due to the build-up of a static electric charge. This is an issue when, for example, shotholes are lined with a plastic sleeve or where rigid plastic containers are used, unless the lining is antistatic.

221 Explosives mixing trucks must be earthed during mixing and transfer operations to dissipate static charges.

222 Delay detonators should be clearly marked with the period of delay when supplied. This period should, preferably, also be marked on the detonator lead.

Shotfiring operations

223 Shotfirers must ensure that shotfiring operations are conducted in accordance with the rules and the blasting specification.

224 Explosives mixed under licence on site must comply with the conditions set out in the licence. They must be mixed where they are to be used and only in sufficient quantities for immediate use.

225 The shotfirer must be fully satisfied that each shothole has been drilled and charged in accordance with the blasting specification. The rise of explosives in holes should be checked at regular intervals to ensure that the shothole is being correctly charged.

226 If it is not possible to conform to the specification, or the danger zone appears to be different from that shown, shotfiring operations should be suspended until any change to the specification has been authorised by its author or other designated person.

227 The shotfirer should only connect a tester to a shotfiring circuit when ready to test or fire the shot. The exploder should be disconnected immediately after firing or in the event of an unsatisfactory test on the firing circuit. No one but the shotfirer should be able to operate the exploder.

228 Workers must obey any relevant instructions in relation to shotfiring operations, for example from the shotfirer or sentry. Sentries are there to keep people out of the danger zone and must not leave their post until the all-clear signal has been given, or until they are released by the person who posted them.

Avoidance of misfires

229 Connections need to be checked immediately before a blast to ensure the integrity of the system and to minimise the risk of a misfire. Where in-hole initiation is used, ie with the detonator placed inside the hole, two detonators are needed for each deck or column of explosives to minimise the possibility of a misfire. This is because faulty detonators cannot be easily identified or recovered.[29]

230 Shock tube connectors need to be covered with enough material to prevent damage to surface lines by shrapnel; about 200 mm of damp dust or chippings is usually enough.

Use of safety fuse

231 Safety fuse needs to be of such quality so that the rate of burning is between 90 and 110 seconds for each metre of fuse. Safety fuse supplied in Britain is likely to meet this standard.

232 It is recommended that a shotfirer should not attempt to ignite more than six lighting points at any one time. When igniter cord is being used to connect lengths of safety fuse, the initiation system should be such that the last length of safety fuse has started to burn before the first detonation occurs.

Safe use of explosives

233 It is recommended that:

(a)   only one container of explosives is open at a shothole at any one time;

(b)   explosives are not used on or inside machinery or used for clearing blockages except where all other means, for example hydraulic breakers, have failed and the explosives are used in accordance with recognised guidance.[30]

234 Explosives should not be taken into a room or other place where people congregate, or where there is a possible source of initiation, for example machinery, electrical equipment or a naked flame.

Charging shotholes etc

235 The shotfirer must be present during charging. Detonators, other explosives and charged holes must not be left unattended. All detonators must be locked in their containers.

236 Any surplus explosives (including detonators) must be removed from the blast area before any attempt is made to fire the shot. The shotfirer must ensure that surplus explosives are not left unattended. They should be returned to the explosives store at the earliest opportunity, not later than the end of the shift, and the records amended accordingly.

Supervision of shotfiring operations and trainee shotfirers and records of appointment

(1)   The operator shall take all reasonable steps to ensure that -

(a)   a trainee shotfirer at the quarry does not fire shots and is not required to fire shots, except when he is under the close personal supervision of a shotfirer, until the operator is satisfied that he has completed a suitable period of training and has appropriate practical experience; and

(b)   all shotfiring operations are carried out under the close personal supervision of the shotfirer.

(2)   The operator shall ensure that a record of the appointment at the quarry of any shotfirer or trainee shotfirer is kept at a suitable place until three years after that shotfirer's or, as the case may be, trainee shotfirer's employment at the quarry ends.

Training of shotfirers

237 All shotfirers must possess sufficient practical and theoretical knowledge and experience to perform their full range of duties. Shotfirers should not be appointed unless they have successfully completed a course of training covering the subjects set out in Appendix 1.

238 A trainee shotfirer must work under the close personal supervision of an experienced shotfirer, with the trainee following a programme of practical instruction by the shotfirer. A written training programme which is given to everyone involved helps ensure that the training is well-structured. The training must continue until the necessary competence has been acquired and demonstrated.

Appointments and authorisations

239 The shotfiring rules should set out arrangements for the appointment of shotfirers, trainee shotfirers and storekeepers and for authorisation of others to work with explosives. The operator, or the blasting contractor if there is one, may make the appointments or authorisations depending on what is required by the rules (see also paragraph 200).

240 As part of ensuring competence, references should be taken up to check that a new shotfirer has sufficient experience and knowledge. An on-site interview and practical test of the applicant's abilities are also needed before anyone is given a job as a shotfirer.

Shotfirer's duties

Before a shot is fired, a shotfirer shall -

> *(a) check the shotfiring system or circuit to ensure that it has been connected correctly;*
>
> *(b) where electrical detonators are used, ensure that they have been correctly connected to the shotfiring system or circuit and that the shotfiring system or circuit is tested with an instrument suitable for the purpose from a position of safety;*
>
> *(c) where appropriate, ensure that the electrical integrity of the shotfiring system or circuit is such as to make a misfire unlikely; and*
>
> *(d) ensure that the shot is fired from a safe place.*

Misfires

In the event of a misfire the operator shall (if this is not the same person) consult the individual appointed under regulation 8(1)(c) and shall ensure, so far as is reasonably practicable, that -

> *(a) apart from himself, no person other than the Explosives Supervisor, shotfirer, trainee shotfirer or any other person authorised by him enters the danger area -*
>
> > *(i) where the shot was fired by means of safety fuse, until a period of 30 minutes has elapsed since the misfire, or*
> >
> > *(ii) where the shot was fired by other means, until a period of 5 minutes has elapsed since the misfire and any shotfiring apparatus has been disconnected from the shot;*
>
> *(b) appropriate steps are taken to determine the cause of and to deal with the misfire; and*
>
> *(c) a suitable record is kept of the misfire.*

Misfires

241   All misfires must be investigated to determine the cause and to enable action to be taken to avoid any recurrence.

242   The blasting specification endorsed with details of any misfire would be a suitable record of misfires.

243   A misfire is reportable to HSE under the Reporting of Injuries, Diseases and Dangerous Occurrences Regulations 1995.[12]

Prohibited activities

> *(1)   No person (other than a person engaged in the transport of explosives to or from the quarry, a shotfirer, trainee shotfirer, a person authorised to handle explosives at a quarry, or a person appointed to be in charge of the explosives store) shall handle explosives at a quarry.*
>
> *(2)   No person shall bring any substance or article (other than explosives) likely to cause an unintended explosion or fire within 10 metres of any explosives or (except for the*

purpose of lighting igniter cord or safety fuse) take any naked flame within 10 metres of any explosives.

(3)   No person shall forcibly remove any detonator lead, safety fuse or other system for initiating shots from a shothole after the shothole has been charged and primed.

(4)   No person shall charge or fire a shot -

(a)   unless there is sufficient visibility to ensure that work preparatory to shotfiring, the shotfiring operation and any site inspection after the shot is fired can be carried out safely;

(b)   in a shothole which has previously been fired, unless he is dealing with a misfire in accordance with action taken in pursuance of regulation 28(b); or

(c)   in any tunnel or other excavation (not being merely a shothole) in the face or side of the quarry for the purpose of extracting minerals or products of minerals.

(5)   No person shall fire a shot -

(a)   unless he is a shotfirer or trainee shotfirer; and

(b)   other than by means of a suitable exploder or suitable safety fuse.

(6)   No person shall cap a safety fuse with a detonator unless he is using equipment designed for the purpose and he is in a suitably sheltered place designated by the operator for the purpose.

244   Only those who have been explicitly appointed or authorised, in accordance with the rules, are allowed to handle explosives in the quarry. Requirements for delivery drivers are covered separately, under the transport legislation (for further information see the transport legislation in paragraph 184).

245   The following methods of shotfiring are prohibited:

(a)   springing - where a succession of gradually increased charges is fired in a shothole to form a cavity or chamber to accommodate a final heavy charge; and

(b)   heading blasts - blasts in any tunnel or other excavation for the purpose of extracting minerals or products of minerals.

Visibility

246   The Quarries (Explosives) Regulations 1988 prohibited blasting between one hour after sunset and one hour before sunrise. This was intended to ensure that there was enough daylight for the blast and other associated work to be carried out safely. This has been replaced with a more general prohibition on blasting when there is not enough visibility to carry out the work safely.

247   Compliance can, largely, be achieved by stating what time a blast may be carried out in the blast specification. The timing should allow for any inspections required before or after the blast. Fog, rain and snow may reduce visibility and make it unsafe to blast. The effect of such factors should be addressed in the shotfiring rules and, if necessary, also in the blast specification.

248   In addition to the visibility considerations, the timing of the blast will be influenced by the nuisance it may create to neighbours. The local authority, usually the Environmental Health Department, can provide advice on this.

General duty to ensure safety of excavations and tips

The operator shall ensure that excavations and tips are designed, constructed, operated and maintained so as to ensure that -

    (a)   instability; or

    (b)   movement,

which is likely to give rise to a risk to the health and safety of any person is avoided.

249 The purpose of this part of these Regulations is to ensure that people, whether working at the quarry or not, are not put at risk because of unsafe excavations or tips. In particular, those in or near the quarry should not be at risk due to the collapse of a quarry face or from the movement of all or part of a tip. The appraisals and assessments, which are explained in the following sections, are tools to ensure this general objective is achieved.

250 The flowchart in Figure 5 (see page 56) explains the relationship between the appraisal and the assessment requirements.

Tips

251 All tips, including stockpiles and lagoons, are covered by these Regulations. It does not matter how big or small they are, what material they are made from, where that material comes from or what will happen to it later. Tips to be used for refilling the excavation or landscaping the site after extraction, stockpiles of materials for later processing or sale, amenity and soil bunds are all covered.

252 Tips include lagoons, whether used for mineral or waste settlement or simply the storage of water. These Regulations cover a wider range of tips at quarries than was covered by the Mines and Quarries (Tips) Act 1969 and the Mines and Quarries (Tips) Regulations 1971.

Excavations

253 The term 'excavation', as used in these Regulations, includes any place at the quarry where minerals are, or have been, extracted, in particular the ground, faces and sides of the quarry, and any other incline, for example access and other cuttings which are not made primarily for winning minerals.

Safety of excavations and tips

254 All excavations and tips, however small, must be designed, constructed and maintained to ensure their safety. The effort expended should be proportionate to the danger the excavation or tip poses. In the case of very small faces or tips, this will usually be minimal. While a full geotechnical assessment is only required on certain excavations and tips, the operator must ensure that they are all properly designed. This involves considering issues such as drainage and the method of construction.

255 The design and operating procedures for excavations and tips must minimise the risk to people in the quarry and those who may be affected by its activities. This includes people who need access to potentially dangerous areas for purposes such as carrying out inspections and assessments. Under regulation 31, key operating procedures must be set out in the rules.

256 It is important to ensure that design, normal operation, inspection, appraisal and assessment work are not carried out in isolation from each other. Information gained from one of these activities needs to be communicated and taken into account in others. For example, if a geotechnical specialist has been involved in design or appraisal, his/her advice should help to draw up the inspection scheme.

257 Any excavation or tip which moves more than was anticipated in its design is potentially unsafe. Emergency procedures should be implemented immediately to determine the risk and appropriate remedial action. This will involve reappraisal or reassessment as soon as possible in accordance with regulations 32 and 33. Such movement may be reportable under the Reporting of Injuries, Diseases and Dangerous Occurrences Regulations 1995 (RIDDOR)[12] (for further information about this aspect of RIDDOR see paragraph 270).

Design of excavations and tips

258 A site investigation* should be carried out before starting a new excavation or large tip. The purpose of this is to ensure a design which is safe and enables safe operation. The relevant matters from Schedule 1 to these Regulations should be addressed as part of the design process.

259 The design should record what relevant data are missing and why. Additional investigations or more cautious design assumptions may be required if the missing information is critical.

260 The design should conform to good engineering practice and relevant standards. Slopes should be designed to provide stability throughout their life. The risk of failure of the excavation or tip should be assessed to ensure the design provides an adequate margin of safety.

261 The design may need to be modified as a result of information obtained during routine working, inspection, appraisal or geotechnical assessment. Simple management procedures are therefore needed to ensure that any such information relevant to the design is reviewed.

262 The limits of where it is safe to excavate or tip should be determined on the basis of the information collected in the site investigation and survey (see Schedule 1 for more information).

263 The design and safety of existing excavations and tips where design data and site information are not available, need to be reviewed as part of the initial appraisal (see regulation 32). Much of the information required for a new design is needed to complete that appraisal satisfactorily.

*Site investigations include desk studies, survey results and any relevant, historical information about the site and its surroundings.

264 Where a proposed excavation or tip is likely to constitute a significant hazard and require a geotechnical assessment under regulation 34, it is strongly recommended that a geotechnical specialist is involved at the design stage. In such cases the initial design, appraisal and assessment may be amalgamated and the design documentation may form the assessment report, provided it addresses the relevant matters from regulation 33 and Schedule 1.

265 The maximum safe height of excavated faces is influenced by the size, height and type of machinery and working methods used. Generally, the lower the face, the easier it is to manage and maintain. Traditionally, a maximum face height of 15 m is preferred where blasting takes place. In other operations the top of the face should be within the reach of the loading equipment.

51

Working excavations and tips

266 Excavations and tips should be developed in accordance with the design. Procedures to ensure proper control of any design changes are essential. These can usefully be explained in the health and safety document or the excavations and tips rules.

267 Working methods must not result in large vertical faces or overhangs, which constitute a significant risk. Reprofiling or digging material from a tip also needs particular care since it may lead to instability.

268 Where material is extracted from beneath water, the edge may collapse into the excavation without warning. The area liable to be affected should be treated as a danger area (regulation 22 gives more information about danger areas). Barriers should be placed around it to keep people out. These must be moved as excavation progresses and the danger area changes.

269 Additional precautions may be required to prevent risks arising where tipping and removal from a stockpile take place simultaneously. For example, a tipping area must not be undermined by removal of material.

270 Under RIDDOR the following incidents are reportable to HSE as dangerous occurrences:

(a) any event (including any movement or fire) which indicates that a tip is, or is likely to become, insecure (ie unsafe); and

(b) any movement or failure of a slope or face which has the potential to cause the death of any person or to adversely affect any building, contiguous land, transport system, footpath, public utility or service, watercourse, reservoir or area of public access.

271 Any movement or failure which could cause death, injury or affect adjacent property, but does not actually do so (for example because it happens outside working hours and no one was present) is reportable.

Stockpiles

272 It is important to remember that the legal term 'tip' includes stockpiles. These can be as dangerous as other tips, and so they too need to be properly designed and operated. The excavations and tips rules are the key to this (see regulation 31). Routine geotechnical assessment is only likely to be necessary for badly placed or large stockpiles.

273 Walls or other supports provided to contain stockpiles are likely to need designing by a competent engineer to ensure their stability. Stockpiles which are not free-draining require adequate drainage.

274 If the market for a product declines significantly, a stockpile may grow dramatically, to an extent that was not anticipated. If this happens, the safety of the stockpile should be subject to a fundamental review. In the past it was often difficult to assess the extent of the associated risk because the original site investigation was limited and tipping was not closely controlled. This ought not to be the case in future, as all tips should be properly designed.

275 Adjacent stockpiles can have an effect on each other, for example stability may be altered where they overlap. The adequacy of traffic routes for vehicles should also be considered when planning the position and size of stockpiles. In particular, the risk of collision can be minimised by ensuring a clear field of view for drivers.

Excavations and tips rules

The operator shall ensure that suitable and sufficient rules (known in these Regulations as the "excavations and tips rules") are made to ensure the safe construction and operation of excavations and tips and such rules shall in particular specify the following matters -

> *(a)   the manner in which such activities are to be carried out;*
>
> *(b)   the nature and extent of supervision of such activities; and*
>
> *(c)   the precautions to be taken during such activities to ensure the health and safety of any person and the safety and stability of the excavation or tip.*

276   These rules are essential for the proper management of excavations and tips. They are the practical measures, or operating procedures, required to keep excavations, tips, and people on and around them, safe. They should therefore provide straightforward practical guidance to those carrying out the excavation work, building the tip and, where appropriate, removing material from a tip.

277   The frequency of inspection of excavations and tips is covered by the inspection scheme required under regulation 12. These inspection arrangements may be incorporated into the rules. These rules do not need to repeat what is in other rules, such as those for vehicles or explosives.

278   If a geotechnical specialist has been involved in the design, or has carried out a geotechnical assessment, it is wise to involve him/her in the preparation of the rules to ensure that they adequately cover all relevant measures.

279   Rules are required for small excavations or tips as well as large ones, but the amount of detail to be included in the rules should be in proportion to the risk posed by the excavation or tip.

280   Rules which cover a number of tips, as opposed to ones which are individually tailored to each tip, may be appropriate if all of the risks can be adequately controlled in this way, and everyone is clear as to what is required for each tip.

281   The rules should specify the way in which the excavation or tip will be constructed and managed to ensure safety. For both excavations and tips they need to address, as relevant:

(a)   the maximum depth/height;

(b)   the preparation necessary (for example the standard of foundations required for a tip);

(c)   the provision of drainage (particularly under, in and on tips) and how it is installed, maintained and inspected;

(d)   the height and slope of faces and the thickness of the layers in which a tip is constructed;

(e)   the type of plant and machinery used;

(f)   the construction standards for roadways and arrangements to prevent tipping vehicles driving or reversing over edges, including the size and shape of edge protection;

(g)   the supervision needed to ensure that work is carried out in accordance with the design and rules;

(h)   what to do if particular defects are found - this should take account of the extent of the defect, the working methods, the nature of the materials and the proximity and vulnerability of neighbouring structures and personnel; and

(i)   the way material may be removed from the excavation or tip, if relevant, including the maximum vertical face height which may be created or left at the end of a working period.

282   The rules for excavations should also address:

(a)   the sequence in which the site will be excavated; and

(b)   the maintenance arrangements for faces, for example mechanical scaling.

283   For solid tips, the degree of compaction required for tipped material should also be considered.

284   In the case of lagoons, the rules also need to address, as relevant:

(a)   the provision of emergency overflows;

(b)   minimum freeboard heights;

(c)   the operation or maintenance of pumps;

(d)   procedures to allow material to be recovered safely from lagoons; and

(e)   procedures when covering lagoons.

Appraisal of excavations and tips

(1)   The operator shall ensure that a suitable and sufficient appraisal of all proposed or existing excavations or tips at the quarry is undertaken by a competent person in order to determine whether any such excavation or tip is a significant hazard.

(2)   The operator shall ensure that -

(a)   any significant findings made during an appraisal, any conclusions reached in accordance with paragraph (1) and the reasons for those conclusions are recorded by the competent person undertaking the appraisal;

(b)   the said competent person signs and dates any such record; and

(c)   the record made in accordance with sub-paragraph (a) is made available to each employer of persons at work at the quarry and to all persons at work at the quarry.

(3)   Where the conclusion reached by the competent person following an appraisal made pursuant to paragraph (1) is that the excavation or tip presents no significant hazard, the operator shall ensure that a competent person carries out further such appraisals -

(a)   at appropriate intervals;

(b)   whenever there is any reason to suspect that there has been or will be a significant change to -

54

(i)   the matters to which the appraisal relates, or

(ii)   any neighbouring land which may be affected by movement by or instability of the excavation or tip to which the appraisal relates; and

(c)   whenever there is any reason to doubt the validity of the conclusion of the current appraisal.

(4)   Where the conclusion reached by the competent person following an appraisal made pursuant to paragraph (1) is that the excavation or tip represents a significant hazard, the operator shall ensure that a geotechnical assessment is carried out in accordance with the requirements of regulation 33 as soon as is reasonably practicable.

Appraisal

285   An appraisal is intended to be a fairly straightforward exercise to determine which excavations and tips, proposed or existing, would pose a significant danger if they failed,* and so merit an assessment by a geotechnical specialist. The relationship between the appraisal and assessment and the elements involved are illustrated in the flowchart in Figure 5 (see page 56).

286   Some appraisals will identify only those hazards from isolated minor failures, such as falls of a single rock or a small amount of sand. A geotechnical assessment does not focus on such hazards. While they may cause deaths, they can be adequately controlled by routine daily inspection, use of appropriate equipment and working methods.

287   The appraisal should be carried out in enough detail and with sufficient expertise to decide, on the basis of the guidance in this section, if an excavation or tip poses a significant hazard from collapse or movement. It is not normally necessary for appraisals to be carried out by a geotechnical specialist, though advice from one is appropriate in cases where the level of hazard is unclear.

288   When carrying out an appraisal there is no need to duplicate work already done, for example under the Management of Health and Safety at Work Regulations 1999 or the previous tips legislation, as long as all the matters detailed in this section are adequately addressed. In some cases it is obvious that any failure of an excavation or tip could kill people, for example an excavation or tip near a public roadway, house or above the quarry offices. In these cases the initial appraisal can be very brief as a geotechnical assessment by a geotechnical specialist will be needed.

289   Areas where no one is directly at risk from a collapse of part of an excavation must be included in the appraisal because failure in such areas could affect the stability of the remainder of the excavation. Appraisal of such areas may also provide information relevant to the safety of other parts of the excavation.

290   Tips which were classified under the Mines and Quarries (Tips) Regulations 1971 will normally need to be subject to routine assessment under these Regulations. In most cases appraisals should conclude that they pose a significant hazard; where this is not the case the conclusion needs clear justification.

291   The appraisal of all excavations and tips must be completed by 1 January 2001. Appraisal of existing classified tips, where no changes are proposed and assessments are still current, can normally rely on existing assessment reports.

* Failure, in this section, includes movement by a tip which is significantly more than that allowed for in the design.

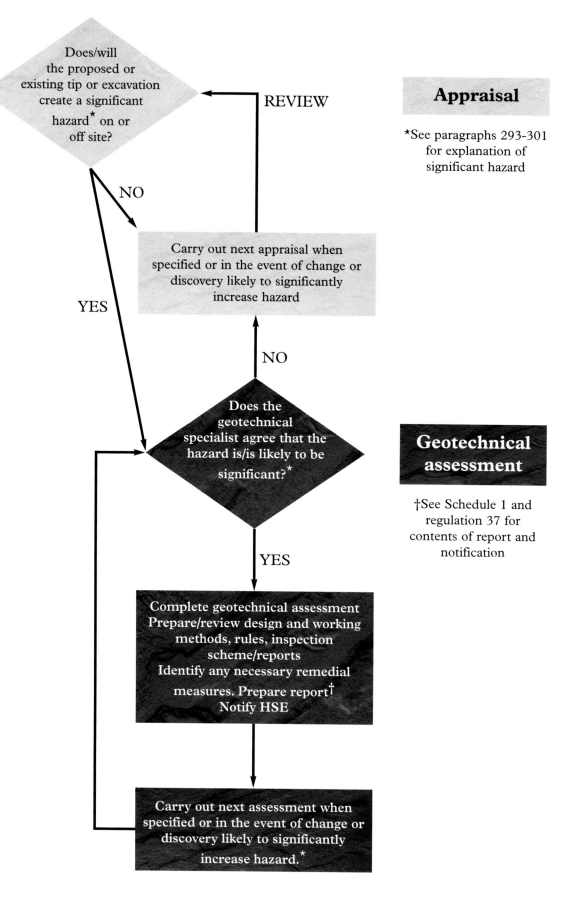

Figure 5 Appraisal and assessment of excavations and tips

292 Among other things, the appraisal should take account of the material to be excavated or tipped, its structure, water content/drainage, the proximity of water courses, roadways, workplaces, residential accommodation, or abandoned workings, and any evidence or history of failures. The matters covered in inspections are also relevant. Appendix 3 provides a model inspection checklist.

Significant hazard

293 To determine if the hazard is significant it is necessary to consider how an excavation or tip might feasibly fail, and the likely consequences of any such failure. The likely consequences are crucial when deciding if a particular hazard is significant. The probability of such a failure actually happening is not relevant in this context.

294 The consequences depend on the likely scale of the failure (ie the size of the failure and the area affected by it) and whether people are likely to be injured.

295 The hazard should be considered significant if such a failure would, directly or indirectly, be:

(a) liable to endanger premises, roadways or other places where people are likely to be found off-site; or

(b) likely to kill or seriously injure anyone.

296 If the degree of hazard is not clear and the excavation or tip is not in the categories described in paragraphs 300 and 301, the advice of a geotechnical specialist should be sought.

297 Where a geotechnical specialist has been involved in design work or in geotechnical assessments he/she may provide written, practical guidance on what constitutes a significant hazard in the context of that particular site. Any such guidance should explain the basis on which it was produced.

298 Such site-specific guidance may be followed for future appraisals, subject to any limitations specified, in preference to the generic guidance in paragraphs 300 and 301. Any such guidance needs to be reviewed in the light of changes or new information.

299 Properly validated analytical techniques for calculating the hazard created by excavations and tips may also be used to determine the significance of the hazard. Such techniques can also be useful in prioritising work.

Tips

300 The hazard should be treated as significant and the tip subject to a geotechnical assessment if it is, or will be:

(a) in a wholly or mainly solid state and not in solution or suspension (ie not likely to flow if not contained); and

    (i) the area of the land covered exceeds 10 000 sq m; or

    (ii) the height of the tip exceeds 15 m; or

(iii)   the average gradient of the land covered by the tip exceeds 1 in 12; or

(b)   a lagoon containing any liquid or material wholly or mainly in solution or suspension (ie likely to flow if not contained); and

(i)   the contents of the lagoon are more than 4 m above the level of any land which is within 50 m of its perimeter; or

(ii)   the contents of the lagoon exceed 10 000 cubic metres; or

(c)   irrespective of the size of the tip, other factors, for example the geology, location or proximity to an excavation, mean that there is a significant hazard as described in paragraphs 293-295.

Excavations

301   The hazard should be treated as significant and the excavation subject to a geotechnical assessment where:

(a)   in the case of moderately weak or stronger rock:*

(i)   the vertical height of any individual face (see Figure 6) is more than 15 m; or

(ii)   the overall vertical height of any adequately benched face or slope, measured from toe to crest (see Figure 6), is between 15 m and 30 m, and the overall face angle is steeper than 1 horizontal to 1 vertical (45° to the horizontal); or

(b)   in the case of weak or very weak rocks and engineering soils, where the vertical height of any part of an excavation is more than 7.5 m, and the overall face angle (see Figure 6) is steeper than 2 horizontal to 1 vertical (27° to the horizontal); or

(c)   the bottom of the excavation is more than 30 m below any surrounding land within 30 m of the perimeter of the excavation (ie the excavation is more than 30 m deep, allowing for any nearby higher ground); or

(d)   irrespective of the excavation face height, depth or angle, other factors, for example the geology, location or proximity of a tip, mean that there is a significant hazard as described in paragraphs 293-295.

Recording and reviewing the appraisal

302   The conclusions of the appraisal should be included in the health and safety document. Where the excavation or tip is considered to be unsafe or likely to become unsafe in the near future, however, there should be a clear recommendation as to what action should be taken and at what point. Little detail need be recorded in other cases where the

---

* The categories of rock are described in British Standard BS 5930. Moderately weak or stronger rock is essentially material which is normally excavated using explosives or saws. Engineering soils and weak or very weak rock are normally extracted using excavators, draglines or other machines.

appraisal is to be followed by a geotechnical assessment. Where there is no significant hazard, the detail should be sufficient to explain the conclusions and how they were reached.

303   The appraisal should be reviewed at appropriate intervals and in particular in the light of:

(a)   significant changes to working methods;

(b)   experience of the geology of the site;

(c)   changes outside the site which significantly increase the hazard, for example the construction of houses or roadways near the boundary;

(d)   evidence of significant failure or movement; or

(e)   discovery of incorrect assumptions or errors in the appraisal.

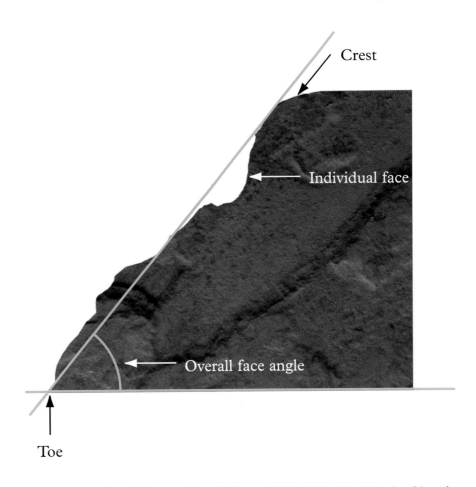

Figure 6 Illustration of the terms 'overall face angle', 'individual face', 'toe' and 'crest'

Meaning of 'geotechnical assessment' and operator's duties in relation to geotechnical assessments

(1)   For the purposes of these Regulations, a "geotechnical assessment" means an assessment carried out by a geotechnical specialist identifying and assessing all factors liable to affect the stability and safety of a proposed or existing excavation or tip and shall include -

(a)   preparation by or under the supervision of the said geotechnical specialist or, as appropriate, consideration by the said geotechnical specialist of the documents and particulars specified at Schedule 1;

(b)   the conclusion of the said geotechnical specialist as to the safety and stability of the proposed or existing excavation or tip being assessed, including his conclusions as to whether the said excavation or tip represents a significant hazard by way of instability or movement;

(c)   where appropriate, the conclusion of the said geotechnical specialist as to whether any remedial work is required in relation to the excavation or tip being assessed and the date by which such work should be completed;

(d)   where appropriate, the conclusion of the said geotechnical specialist as to the date by which the next geotechnical assessment should take place; and

(e)   consideration by the said geotechnical specialist of the excavations and tips rules.

(2)   The operator shall ensure that -

(a)   any significant findings made during a geotechnical assessment and any conclusions reached in accordance with paragraphs (1)(b), (c) or (d) and the reasons for those conclusions are recorded by the geotechnical specialist undertaking the assessment; and

(b)   the said geotechnical specialist signs and dates any such record and records his professional qualifications thereon.

(3)   The operator shall ensure that any information available to him which may be relevant for the purposes of a geotechnical assessment is made available to the geotechnical specialist undertaking that assessment.

(4)   The operator shall ensure that any remedial works identified during the geotechnical assessment in accordance with paragraph (1)(c) are undertaken by the date specified.

Geotechnical assessment

304   The geotechnical assessment should cover similar topics to the appraisal, but in greater depth and in more detail. All relevant parts of Schedule 1 must be addressed. The appraisal concentrates on the hazard posed by an excavation or tip; the assessment should also pay particular attention to the risk of failure.

305   Where required, the first geotechnical assessment for all excavations and tips must be completed by 1 January 2002 (see regulation 1(2)). For tips that were classified under the Mines and Quarries (Tips) Regulations 1971, see regulation 38.

306 It is important to ensure that design, normal operation, inspection, appraisal and assessment work are not carried out in isolation from each other. Information gained as a result of all these activities needs to be shared.

307 The report needs to be presented in a form that will help the operator to manage the safe development of the excavation or tip, and to organise appropriate inspections.

ACOP

308 General guidance on what constitutes a significant hazard is contained in paragraphs 293-295. The types of tips listed in paragraph 300 come from the definition of a classified tip in the 1971 Regulations. This definition has stood the test of time, and such tips normally present a significant hazard. Operators need to ensure that geotechnical specialists who conclude that such a tip is not a significant hazard clearly explain and record the basis for their judgement. Where a tip is near the crest of an excavation then the tip and the excavation must be considered together.

Geotechnical specialist

309 The level of expertise required to carry out a geotechnical assessment depends on the complexity of the site and properties of the material being worked or tipped. The geotechnical specialist must have sufficient expertise and practical experience of similar conditions to adequately assess the safety of the excavation or tip, and the precautions required to make and keep it safe.

310 The operator must ensure that any remedial work identified during a geotechnical assessment is carried out by the date specified by the geotechnical specialist. When deciding how long to allow for remedial measures, the geotechnical specialist should consider the risk involved. The greater the risk, the sooner the work needs to be completed.

Regulation 34

Operator's duties in relation to excavations and tips which are a significant hazard ('notifiable' excavations and tips)

Regulation

(1) Where the conclusion recorded by a geotechnical specialist in accordance with regulation 33(1)(b) following a geotechnical assessment of a proposed or existing excavation or tip is that the excavation or tip represents a significant hazard by way of instability or movement, the operator shall ensure, subject to regulation 33(1)(d), that the said excavation or tip is subject to a further geotechnical assessment at least every two years.

(2) Without prejudice to paragraph (1), where, in relation to an excavation or tip which falls within paragraph (1) there is any reason -

(a) to suspect that there has been or will be a significant change to -

(i) the matters to which the geotechnical assessment relates; or

(ii) any neighbouring land which may be affected by movement by or instability of the excavation or tip; or

(b) to doubt the validity of the conclusion of the current assessment,

the operator shall ensure that a further geotechnical assessment is undertaken as soon as is reasonably practicable.

(3) For the purposes of these Regulations, excavations and tips falling within paragraph (1) shall be known as "notifiable excavations" and "notifiable tips" respectively.

311 Excavations and tips that constitute a significant hazard (see paragraphs 293-295) must be subject to geotechnical assessment at least once every two years. The date by which the next geotechnical assessment is to be carried out must be specified in the geotechnical specialist's report.

312 Some excavations and tips will require frequent geotechnical assessments. A three-monthly review of the geotechnical assessment is normally appropriate for tips, including spoilheaps and backfill, where large quantities of material are deposited at a high rate, for example at most opencast coal sites.

Review

313 Further geotechnical assessments must be carried out as specified by the geotechnical specialist (and at least every two years) or in the event of:

(a)   significant changes to working methods;

(b)   new information about the geology of the site;

(c)   changes outside the site which significantly increase the hazard, for example the construction of houses or roadways near the boundary;

(d)   evidence of significant failure or movement; or

(e)   discovery of incorrect assumptions or errors in the assessment.

314 Wherever possible, such assessments should be undertaken before any significant change, but where this is not possible they must take place as soon as reasonably practicable.

315 A change to the excavation or tip itself, for example in design, method of working or material tipped, may significantly increase the hazard. In such cases a further geotechnical assessment must be carried out. This may also be required if fundamental assumptions in the geotechnical assessment are found to be incorrect, for example regarding the geology of the site.

316 A new development on land adjacent to an excavation or tip, for example the construction of a school, housing estate or road, could significantly increase the hazard. Such changes are likely to be known well in advance and should be planned for.

Reworking tips

317 Tips which are subject to routine geotechnical assessment may be worked or used for landscaping. It is normally appropriate to consult a geotechnical specialist when planning such operations, since dangerous movement is more likely to take place when a tip is disturbed.

Operator's duties in relation to excavations and tips which are not a significant hazard

Where the conclusion reached by a geotechnical specialist in accordance with regulation 33(1)(b) following a geotechnical assessment of a proposed or existing excavation or tip is that it presents no significant hazard, the operator shall ensure that -

(a)   the said geotechnical specialist specifies the frequency with which appraisals pursuant to regulation 32 are to be conducted in order to

ensure the continued safety and stability of the excavation or tip; and

(b)   a record of that specification is made.

Low-hazard tips

318   In some cases the hazard from even large tips may be extremely low, for example tips:

(a)   which have been landscaped and present no danger;

(b)   which are immediately surrounded on all sides by higher, stable ground, so that it is not possible for the tipped material to move; and

(c)   where an exemption was granted under the previous legislation.

Such tips are not likely to require geotechnical assessment.

319   Some such tips may no longer be on quarry premises, for example if they are part of a farm or industrial development. Such tips are not subject to these Regulations, and the only duty on the quarry operator is to make sure they are safe when they are handed over to the farmer or developer. Since this does not mean that a tip could not later become unsafe, any information which might help a purchaser to identify and avoid risks needs to be passed on.

320   Tips to which these Regulations do not apply may be subject to the requirements in Part II of the Mines and Quarries (Tips) Act 1969. For further information see paragraph 353.

Regulation 36

Duty to keep record of substances tipped

The operator shall ensure that sufficient records are kept of the nature, quantity and location of all substances accumulated or deposited at a notifiable tip to enable an accurate assessment of the stability of that tip to be made.

321   Records of the material deposited may be kept electronically or on paper. The layout of the records should be clear and unambiguous, but their design is left to the discretion of the operator. The quantity of material deposited is normally recorded as the uncompacted volume in cubic metres. If another method is preferred, this should be clear and applied consistently.

322   This information is needed throughout the life of a notifiable tip, and so it should be kept until there is no prospect of further tipping, or excavation on or near the tip. The quarry owner may also require the information after this time, to meet the requirements in Part II of the Mines and Quarries (Tips) Act 1969. For further information see paragraph 353.

Regulation 37

Notification of excavations and tips

(1)   Subject to paragraph (2), the operator shall in relation to any -

(a)   proposed excavation or tip which it is reasonable to expect will be a significant hazard;

(b)   notifiable excavation; or

(c)   notifiable tip other than a notifiable tip which was -

(i)   a classified tip within the meaning of regulation 2(1) of the 1971 Regulations, and

(ii)   in respect of which notice has been given in accordance with regulation 8(1) of those Regulations,

give not less than 30 days notice (or such shorter period as the Executive may permit) to the Executive of his intention to commence or, in relation to excavations and tips falling within sub-paragraphs (b) and (c), continue, operations.

(2)   Paragraphs (1)(b) and (1)(c) shall not apply to an excavation or tip in relation to which notice of intention to commence operations has previously been given.

(3)   The 30 days notice referred to in paragraph (1) shall be given -

(a)   in the case of excavations and tips falling within paragraph (1)(a), before the commencement of operations; and

(b)   in the case of excavations and tips falling within paragraphs (1)(b) and (1)(c), as soon as possible after the date on which the operator is notified of the geotechnical specialist's conclusions, reached in accordance with regulation 33(1)(b).

(4)   The following information shall be included in any notice given by the operator in accordance with paragraph (1) -

(a)   a brief description of the excavation or tip, including its location, size, and the material to be excavated or tipped; and

(b)   in relation to excavations and tips falling within paragraphs (1)(b) and (1)(c), the conclusions reached by the geotechnical specialist carrying out the geotechnical assessment in accordance with paragraphs (1)(b), (c) and (d) of regulation 33.

(5)   Where the conclusion reached by a geotechnical specialist during the geotechnical assessment of an excavation or tip which has, in accordance with regulation 34(1), been subject to a geotechnical assessment at least every two years is that the excavation or tip no longer presents a significant hazard by way of instability or movement, the operator shall give notice of that conclusion and the reasons for that conclusion to the Executive within two months of the geotechnical assessment.

323   If the operator judges that a new excavation or tip is likely to create a significant hazard, he/she must inform HSE at least 30 days before starting excavation or tipping. Notification is not required where HSE has already been notified of a classified tip under the Mines and Quarries (Tips) Regulations 1971.

324   In the case of excavations and of existing tips which were not previously classified, the operator must inform HSE within 30 days of a geotechnical specialist concluding that they are a significant hazard.

325   The notification must include a brief description (two to three lines) of the proposed or existing excavation or tip, its location (including the Ordnance Survey grid reference), the geotechnical specialist's conclusion regarding the risk and the proposed frequency of geotechnical assessment. Where there are several notifiable excavations or tips on the same site, a single, combined notification for all of them is sufficient.

326   Operators must also inform HSE when a geotechnical specialist concludes that a previously notified excavation or tip no longer presents a significant hazard. They must include a brief explanation of the reduction in the hazard. Routine appraisal of such excavations or tips must continue at intervals determined by the geotechnical specialist.

Regulation 38

Transitional provisions

Where, at the coming into force of these Regulations, a report has been obtained in accordance with regulations 9(2)(a), 12(1) or 18(1) of the 1971 Regulations and is less than two years old, that report shall be treated as a geotechnical assessment for the purpose of regulation 32(4) of these Regulations and shall remain valid for a maximum of two years from the date when it was first made.

327 Reports obtained in accordance with regulations 9, 12 or 18 of the Mines and Quarries (Tips) Regulations 1971 satisfy the requirement for a geotechnical assessment. These reports remain valid for a maximum of two years from the date when they were first made. They should be kept with any new assessment reports as they will provide much of the required background information.

Regulation 39

Co-operation

Every employer of persons at work at a quarry and every person at work at the quarry shall co-operate with the operator to the extent requisite to enable the operator to comply with the relevant statutory provisions.

Guidance

328   In many quarries much of the work is carried out by contractors. Such contractors may be large or small companies or self-employed individuals.

329   Regulation 11 of the Management of Health and Safety at Work Regulations 1999 requires co-operation and co-ordination between these contractors. This regulation extends that duty by requiring all contractors and the workforce to co-operate with the operator. Contractors also have duties under regulation 12 of the Management of Health and Safety at Work Regulations 1999 to those not employed by them who work in parts of the quarry under their control.

330   Good co-operation and co-ordination is crucial to ensuring health and safety and for the operator to fulfil the duties under these Regulations to:

(a)   compile the health and safety document;

(b)   manage the quarry in a co-ordinated way which ensures health and safety; and

(c)   ensure that the health and safety arrangements described in the health and safety document work in practice.

331   The development of the health and safety document and its effective implementation depend on the flow of information between the operator, the contractors and the workforce.

332   Contractors must tell the operator about any injuries, diseases and dangerous occurrences that are reportable under RIDDOR.[12] This is so that the operator can make the necessary notifications to HSE, and ensure that the arrangements for managing health and safety and controlling risks are appropriate (for more information about reviewing health and safety measures see regulation 11).

Regulation 40

Participation of persons at work

(1)   It shall be the duty of the operator to make and maintain arrangements which will enable him and those persons who regularly work at the quarry to co-operate effectively in promoting and developing measures to ensure the health, safety and welfare of persons who regularly work at the quarry and in checking the effectiveness of such measures.

(2)   For the purposes described in paragraph (1), a committee of persons with suitable practical experience of quarrying operations may be appointed for the quarry -

(a)   in a case where there is an association or body representative of a majority of the total number of persons working at the quarry, by that association or body; or

(b)   jointly by associations or bodies which are together representative of such a majority.

(3) Where an injury or dangerous occurrence which is notifiable under the Reporting of Injuries, Diseases and Dangerous Occurrences Regulations 1995[(a)] occurs at a quarry, the operator shall permit two members of the committee appointed under paragraph (2) to inspect together the place where the injury or dangerous occurrence occurred and, so far as is necessary for ascertaining its cause, any other part of the quarry and any plant, and to take samples of the atmosphere, dust or water at that place.

(4) The operator of a quarry shall permit sufficient inspections to be carried out by members of the committee appointed under paragraph (2) to enable every part of the quarry and any plant and equipment at the quarry to be inspected once a month by two of those committee members together.

(5) The operator of a quarry shall permit members of a committee appointed under paragraph (2) who are carrying out an inspection under paragraph (4) to -

(a) scrutinise any documents which are kept at the quarry in compliance with the relevant statutory provisions;

(b) review the risk assessment referred to in regulation 7(1)(a) and the measures referred to in regulation 7(1)(b) and to suggest improvements thereto; and

(c) be accompanied by their advisers.

(6) The operator of a quarry shall ensure that any improvements suggested under paragraph (5)(b) are considered and, if they are not accepted, written reasons for this are given to the members of the committee who made the inspection.

(7) The operator of a quarry and any person nominated by him shall be entitled to accompany the two committee members appointed under paragraph (2) who are carrying out an inspection under paragraph (4) during that inspection.

(8) Where any two committee members appointed under paragraph (2) have carried out an inspection under paragraph (4), they may make a written report of the matters ascertained as a result of the inspection and, if such a report is made, the two committee members and the operator or any person nominated by him shall sign the report.

(9) Where a written report is made, a copy of the report signed in accordance with paragraph (8) shall be posted in a conspicuous position at the quarry and kept posted there for 28 days.

(a) SI 1995/3163 to which there are amendments not relevant to these Regulations.

40

333 This regulation should be read in conjunction with:

(a) the Health and Safety (Consultation with Employees) Regulations 1996;[31] and

(b) the Safety Representatives and Safety Committees Regulations 1977[32] as amended by the Management of Health and Safety at Work Regulations 1999.

334 The involvement of the entire workforce in identifying and controlling the risks is crucial to the reduction of the high accident rate associated with quarrying. The establishment of an active safety committee is a highly effective way of encouraging the co-operation and participation of the whole workforce in the safe management of the quarry and to improve standards of health and safety. To be successful, the committee must be seen by all parties as being effective.

40

Guidance

40

335 Committee members should have suitable practical experience of quarry work, and may represent any section of the workforce at the quarry. A single committee covering the whole quarry or even a group of quarries is generally appropriate. In a small quarry the committee may involve every member of the workforce.

Site inspections

336 Site inspections provide a way in which the workforce can be actively involved in practical site safety. Their detailed knowledge of the site and working practices can lead to significant improvements in health and safety. These inspections are best carried out jointly by a team representing the management and those working in the quarry, and the findings discussed and minuted at safety committee meetings.

Encouraging active participation

337 The team approach to health and safety can also be fostered by actively involving people in managing the hazards associated with their work. For example, it is best to include those affected when developing new systems; their involvement in equipment trials helps identify the best solution and can avoid expensive mistakes.

Regulation 41

Regulation

41

Duty of employers of employees at work at a quarry

(1)   No employer shall employ any person to work at a quarry unless there is an operator.

(2)   Without prejudice to regulation 6, where the employees of more than one employer are at work at a quarry, it shall be the duty of each employer to comply with those relevant statutory provisions which apply to the quarry.

Guidance

41

338 The duties on the operator under these Regulations do not relieve individual employers of their duty to comply with other statutory duties. For example, an employer using work equipment, eg vehicles, must comply with the provisions of PUWER, even though the operator has duties under the Quarries Regulations 1999 to prepare vehicles rules and provide edge protection.

339 There can only be one operator for each quarry, and it is very important that this role is clearly allocated. If there are several employers who could be the operator, or it is not clear which of them is in overall control, then they must agree among themselves who will take overall control, or divide the excavation into several quarries, each with its own operator.

Regulation 42

Regulation

42

Duty of persons at work at a quarry

Every person at work at a quarry shall -

(a)   to the extent of his responsibility and authority, carry out the duties allocated to him with reasonable care for the health and safety of himself and other persons who may be affected by his acts or omissions; and

(b)   comply with the rules put in place at the quarry by the operator in accordance with regulation 10.

340 Health and safety at a quarry can only be achieved if everyone understands that the lives of others are in their hands. All those working at the quarry have a part to play, and must do their job carefully and comply with rules required by these Regulations.

341 Anyone who identifies a significant risk, for example because procedures or rules are not followed or where safeguards are missing or inadequate, must take appropriate action, normally by reporting it to a supervisor.

Regulation 43

Health surveillance

An employer of a person at work at a quarry shall ensure, where health surveillance under regulation 5 of the 1992 Regulations is required in respect of any work to which that person is to be assigned, that the health surveillance commences before that person begins to carry out such work.

342 Regulation 6 of the Management of Health and Safety at Work Regulations 1999 and regulation 11 of the Control of Substances Hazardous to Health Regulations 1999 require employers to provide appropriate health surveillance for their employees, having regard to the risks they face.

343 The requirement in these Regulations for pre-employment medicals is in addition to the existing post-employment health surveillance, but is required in the same circumstances.* Health surveillance is also required when anyone transfers to a new job within the quarry if this means that they will be exposed to a different health risk, for example if they begin work in a dusty or noisy area.

344 Conducting health surveillance on someone before they begin to carry out a particular task provides a starting point from which to determine the effect of health risks at the quarry. This can ensure that adverse health effects are detected at an early stage.

* General guidance on health surveillance in quarrying is available from the Quarry Products Association.

Record keeping

(1) It shall be the duty of the operator to ensure that -

(a) every report or record which is required to be made under these Regulations is in a suitable form and is kept at the quarry or at some other suitable place for at least three years from the date on which the report or record was made unless the provision concerned expressly imposes some other requirement; and

(b) a copy of the written statement of duties of all persons appointed at the quarry under these Regulations is kept at the quarry or at some other suitable place for at least 12 months after the date on which the appointment ceased to have effect.

(2) Paragraph (1)(a) shall apply to copies of information notified to the Executive under these Regulations but shall not apply to the record made in accordance with regulation 5(2) by the person entitled to work the quarry.

345 The information contained in the documents required under these Regulations must be kept available for at least three years. This provides data from which operators can identify and monitor trends and make judgements, for example about plant maintenance. The retention of records also enables them to be examined by HSE inspectors.

346 The way in which records are made and stored is left to the discretion of the operator, but the information needs to be stored accurately and to be easily retrievable. Records may be kept electronically (with suitable backup arrangements) or on paper.

347 The records may be kept anywhere, provided that anyone who has a right to see them can readily obtain them, for example by electronic transmission.

Table 3 Records required under these Regulations

Record	Regulation
Inspection records	12(1)(b)
Flammable/explosive atmospheres	21(1)(c)
Appointments	
Quarry manager	8(1)(c)
Managers, supervisors etc	8(1)(e)
Explosives supervisor	25(1)(b)
Shotfirers, storekeepers etc	26(2)
Misfires	28(c)
Blasting specifications	25(2)(b)
Conclusions of appraisals and assessments	32(2)(a)
	33(2)(a)
Substances tipped	36

348 Other documents are required in these Regulations, for example the health and safety document (regulation 7) and one outlining the management structure (regulation 8). These are required to be available and up to date; old versions do not have to be kept for three years. Table 3 summarises the records required under these Regulations and the corresponding regulation reference.

Notification of quarrying operations

(1)   It shall be the duty of the operator to ensure that within 14 days of any of the events specified at paragraphs (a) to (c) of paragraph (2), written notice thereof is given to the Executive.

(2)   The events referred to at paragraph (1) are -

(a)   the beginning of operations for the purpose of opening a quarry;

(b)   the abandonment of or ceasing of operations at a quarry; and

(c)   the appointment or change of the operator of a quarry.

(3)   Without prejudice to the duty to give notice under paragraph (1) in respect of an event specified at paragraph (2)(b), the operator of every quarry of coal shall, within three months of the date on which the quarry of coal is abandoned, send to the Executive, or a body approved by it, an accurate plan of that quarry.

(4)   Where, in pursuance of paragraph (2), a plan has been sent to the Executive or a body approved by it, that plan shall be retained by the Executive or that body in accordance with arrangements approved by the Executive.

45

349   Notification should be sent to the local HSE office when operations for opening a quarry begin. Such operations include putting in roads, clearing topsoil or building offices and workshops. Operators must also notify HSE when a quarry is abandoned.

350   On opening a quarry, there is no particular form to use when notifying HSE of any of the events noted in paragraph 349, but the notification must be in writing and include:

(a)   the name and address of the operator of the quarry;

(b)   the name and address of the quarry (including the post code);

(c)   the telephone and fax number of the quarry;

(d)   the Ordnance Survey grid reference;

(e)   a brief description of the quarry and mineral to be extracted; and

(f)   the date when extraction of minerals is expected to start.

351   When a coal quarry is abandoned, the operator should send the Coal Authority the following:

(a)   the name of the operator and owner (see paragraph 31 for more information about the legal responsibilities of the owner) and the address where notices may be served on them;

(b)   the name of the quarry; and

(c)   scale diagrams of the quarry showing:

(i)   the Ordnance Survey national grid reference;

(ii)   the extent of the working area, including the extent of any auguring;

45

(iii)   the terminal depth;

(iv)   the position of the quarry and that of nearby quarries and mines relative to each other;

(v)   the location of slurry lagoons; and

(vi)   old shafts and workings encountered and not previously recorded.

352   HSE finds it helpful to be notified when the name of the operator or quarry is changed. Operators may also need to notify the utility companies when this happens. There have been delays during emergencies when the power to a quarry needed to be cut off, but the name for the quarry used by the quarry personnel and the electricity supplier was different.

353   When a quarry closes, any remaining excavations or tips must be left in a safe condition (see regulation 6(4)). Tips as defined in the Mines and Quarries (Tips) Act 1969 will, on abandonment of the quarry, become Part II tips under that Act, which is enforced through the Environmental Protection Act 1990. HSE should be notified of the quarry closure (see regulation 45).

354   In the case of such tips, the abandonment notification needs to include the information gathered during geotechnical assessments. This information will be passed on to local authorities who are responsible for enforcing Part II of the Mines and Quarries (Tips) Act 1969.

Exemptions

(1)   Subject to paragraph (2), the Executive may, by a certificate in writing, exempt any quarry, part of a quarry or class of quarries, any person or class of persons, any plant or class of plant or any operation or class of operations from all or any of the prohibitions and requirements of these Regulations, and any such exemption may be granted subject to conditions and to a limit of time and may be revoked at any time by a certificate in writing.

(2)   The Executive shall not grant any such exemption unless, having regard to the circumstances of the case and in particular to -

(a)   the conditions, if any, it proposes to attach to the exemption; and

(b)   any other requirements imposed by or under any enactment which apply to the case,

it is satisfied that the health and safety of persons who are likely to be affected by the exemption will not be prejudiced in consequence of it.

Regulation 47

Repeals and modifications

(1)   The provisions of the 1954 Act specified in column 1 of Part 1 of Schedule 2 are repealed to the extent specified in the corresponding entry in column 3 of that Part.

(2)   The provisions of the 1954 Act specified in column 1 of Part II of Schedule 2 shall not apply to quarries and accordingly those provisions shall be modified to the extent specified in the corresponding entry in column 2 of that Part.

(3)   The provision of the Factories Act 1961[(a)] specified in column 1 of Schedule 3 shall be modified to the extent specified in the corresponding entry in column 2 of that Schedule.

(4)   The provisions of the 1969 Act specified in column 1 of Part I of Schedule 4 shall be modified to the extent specified in the corresponding entry in column 2 of that Part.

(5)   The provisions of the 1969 Act specified in column 1 of Part II of Schedule 4 shall not apply to quarries and accordingly those provisions shall be modified to the extent specified in column 2 of that Part.

47

(a) 1961 c.34 to which there are amendments not relevant to these Regulations.

Guidance

355 The Workplace (Health, Safety and Welfare) Regulations 1992 were amended by the Quarries Miscellaneous Health and Safety Provisions Regulations 1995. The 1995 Regulations applied the 1992 Workplace Regulations to quarries from 26 July 1998, except for regulation 12 which, at a quarry, applies only to traffic routes inside buildings.

356 Although these Regulations repeal the Quarries Miscellaneous Health and Safety Provisions Regulations, the Workplace Regulations continue to apply in quarries as before.

47

Regulation 48

Revocations and modifications to instruments

(1)   The instruments specified in column 1 of Part I of Schedule 5 shall be revoked to the extent specified in the corresponding entry in column 3 of that Part.

(2)   The provisions of the instruments specified in column 1 of Part II of Schedule 5 shall be modified to the extent specified in the corresponding entry in column 2 of that Part.

48

Content of geotechnical assessments

Regulation 33(1)(a)

Site survey

1   An accurate plan which should be prepared on a scale not less detailed than 1:2500 showing -

(a)   *the boundaries of the quarry or premises upon which the excavation or tip or proposed excavation or tip is or is to be situated;*

(b)   *the site of the excavation or tip or proposed excavation or tip;*

(c)   *any contiguous land or structures which might be affected by the excavation or tip or proposed excavation or tip; and*

(d)   *all mine workings (whether abandoned or not), buried quarry workings, known cave systems, active or former landslips, springs, artesian wells, watercourses and other natural or man-made features including tunnel pipes or culverts which might affect the safety of the excavation or tip or proposed excavation or tip or which might be relevant for the purpose of determining whether excavation or tipping operations can be carried out safely,*

which plan shall be contoured to Ordnance Datum Newlyn at a vertical interval not greater than 5 metres and orientated to and correlated with the Ordnance Survey National Grid and marked with squares corresponding to the 100 metre squares shown on Ordnance Survey sheets on the scale of 1:2500.

Site investigation

2   A record of all relevant site investigation information including surveys, tests, boreholes and groundwater measurements made for the purpose of the geotechnical assessment together with the results of any testing including the strength of materials within and beneath the tip or within the excavated slope. The record shall include any known historical information relevant to the site investigation.

Cross-sections based on site investigation

3   Sufficient accurate cross-sections on a scale not less detailed than 1:1250 of the site of the excavation or tip or proposed excavation or tip showing the existing ground surface and all relevant superficial materials and bedrock underlying the said site and -

(a)   *any variation in the thickness, level or character of the superficial deposits and bedrock materials based on the site investigation; and*

(b)   *the position of any surface whether natural or manmade which may affect the safety of the excavation or tip or proposed excavation or tip.*

Plans based on site investigation

4   Plans showing the position of all boreholes, wells and trial pits used in the site investigation and the location and levels of all materials and surfaces which may affect the safety of the excavation or tip or proposed excavation or tip.

Assumptions made before analysis

5   *A record of any assumptions relevant to the assessment of ground conditions relating to the safety of the excavation or tip made by the geotechnical specialist including a record of any relevant information which was not available when undertaking the assessment.*

Findings of analysis

6   *A record of the calculations carried out in order to determine the safety of the excavation or tip, including any variables or parameters used in those calculations and the reasons for using them and the findings of those calculations expressed as the factor of safety or the probability of failure or other recognised basis of assessing stability.*

Design coming out of analysis

7   *An accurate plan on a scale not less detailed than 1:2500 recording -*

   (a)   in relation to tips or proposed tips, the design of the tip, including the area of land covered or to be covered, the gradients of that land, the designed contours at vertical intervals of not more than 2 metres, the side slopes and boundaries of the tip and the designed position and nature of construction of any wall or other structure retaining or confining the tip; and

   (b)   in relation to excavations or proposed excavations, the design of the excavation, including the height or proposed height of the slope, the position and width of any benches and representative contours of the excavation at vertical intervals of not more than 5 metres.

Requirements during and after construction

8   *A record of the nature and extent of inspection, supervision and safety measures necessary to ensure the safety of the excavation or tip and a specification of necessary engineering works and safety measures. A record of the action to be taken regarding defects specified in the report.*

Training course for shotfirers

On completion of a course, shotfirers should be able to demonstrate an adequate understanding of the types of explosives, detonators and shotfiring equipment available, their characteristics, properties and the following topics:

On-site mixed explosives

Practical requirements of HSE licences

Storage, issue, conveyance of explosives and detonators

Recognition, handling and safe disposal of deteriorated explosives including detonators

Design

Blast specification

Prevention of flyrock

Determination of the danger zone

Drilling

Methods and equipment

The plotting of profiles of the face

Setting up and alignment of drills

Checking and measurement of drill holes

Recognition of natural joints and other relevant information from drill holes

Shotfiring operations

Safe shotfiring procedure, warning and shelter

Methods of primary and secondary blasting

Inspection and measurement of quarry faces

Factors affecting vibration and projection of material

Stemming of shotholes

Methods of initiation

Testing of equipment and circuits

Examination of the blast site after firing

Relevant legislation and guidance material

Misfires and methods of dealing with them.

Blasting specification

The following matters need to be addressed when planning, preparing for and undertaking a blast:

1   The part of the quarry where minerals are to be broken up or loosened by the blast, shown on a plan.

2   The intended hole positions, marked on a drilling plan, showing the length, diameter and the angle of inclination and direction at which the drill is to be set for each hole.

3   The surface position* and number or other identifier for each shothole.

4   The angle of inclination, direction, length and diameter and the extent of any sub-grade drilling for each completed shothole.

5   Where the minerals form a face, the profiles or other data required to determine the burden around each shothole.

6   Any geological anomalies which could affect the blast, in particular those identified during drilling and inspection. These might include the presence of cavities, clay bands, joint planes, bedding planes or discontinuities.

7   Using the available information, particularly that from items 4, 5 and 6, shown using plans and sections, the burden for each shothole should be determined and consequently the amount, type and placement of explosives to be used, so that the blast can be carried out safely.

8   The amount, type and position of explosives, the description and position of any detonator and the type and position of any stemming actually used for each shothole.

9   The system of initiation, including full details of any delay sequence and timing.

10   The danger zone, shotfiring position and sentry positions should be determined. (These may be marked on the plan prepared for item 1.)

11   The visibility and other precautions required to minimise the risk of:

(a)   material being projected by the blast;

(b)   misfires; and

(c)   injury during inspection of the site before and after the blast.

12   The date and timing of the blast and prevailing weather conditions.

The blast specification should record information on all of these issues.

---

* The position needs to be identified with sufficient accuracy to enable the explosives to be located in the event of a misfire. Positions can be indicated: on a plan, relative to one or more identified fixed points or using co-ordinates obtained, for example, using the Global Positioning System (GPS).

Excavation and tip inspection reports

The following checklist and report form is a model which can be tailored to the needs of a particular quarry. It is not intended to be used as it stands.

Site		Weather	Last inspected	Date

Condition of excavated face/tip	Feature observed		Details of condition and location
Crests	Yes	No	Details
Lowering of ground surface at or behind the crest of the overall slope/bench			
Cracking behind the crest of the overall slope/bench			
Water running over the crest of the overall slope/bench			
Water entering cracks behind the crest of the overall slope/bench			
New accumulations of water behind the crest of the overall slope/bench			
Surcharging of ground behind the crest of the overall slope/bench			
Face	Yes	No	Details
Bulging of the slope face			
Settlement of slope face			
Displacement across joints/bedding planes etc			
Open structural features inclined > 10 degrees out of the face			
Open structural features inclined steeply > 70 degrees out of the face			
Loose material on the face			
Irregular slope gradient			
Irregularities in plan of the slope face			
Water issuing from the face			
Drainage blankets blocked			
Toe	Yes	No	Details
Ground movements at or in front of the toe of the overall slope/bench			
Water issuing from or in front of the toe of the overall slope/bench			
New accumulation of water at the toe of the overall slope/bench			
Excavations at or near toe of structure not as per design of quarry/tip			

Site		Weather		Last inspected	Date

Condition of excavated face/tip	Feature observed		Details of condition and location	

Water courses/lagoons behind crest	Yes	No	Details
Wave erosion of embankment/bank erosion			
Inflow, outflow or storm overflow impeded			
Is freeboard less than specified in tipping rules?			
Signs of damage due to animals			
Escape of material in suspension or solution			
Indications of silting			
Impending or partial blockages			
Other observations	**Yes**	**No**	**Details**
Adverse drainage from access roads			
Indications of recent ground movements			
Construction varying from plan or tipping rules			
Instruments damaged, recording movements, or rises in water level			
Recent or active rockfall			
Recent or active slope failure			
Unexpected geological conditions appeared since last inspection			
Other changes in slope condition or features of note			
Indications of burning			
Variations from design			
Benches and haul roads	**Yes**	**No**	**Details**
Are the benches and haul roads stable and without signs of failure?			
Any changes to the quarry geology or slope conditions that may affect stability?			
Are haul roads of adequate width and safe gradient?			
Are there excessive ruts, potholes or bumps?			
Is edge protection adequate?			
Has the approved excavation procedure been followed?			
Are quarry loading areas of adequate size?			

Comments	Action required

Safety and stability of the excavated slopes/tips

Recommendations for immediate action

Signed...Date ....

Recommendations agreed or varied

Signed...Date ....

Action taken to remedy defects

Signed...(Quarry Manager)

Note: This model inspection form can be downloaded from
http://www.open.gov.uk/hse/spd/tipform.doc
It can be edited to meet individual requirements.

Vehicle safety in quarries

Introduction

1   The largest single group of fatal and serious quarry accidents involves vehicles. A multi-faceted approach is needed to significantly reduce this toll. It must address all the risk factors and people involved. This is illustrated in Figure 7.

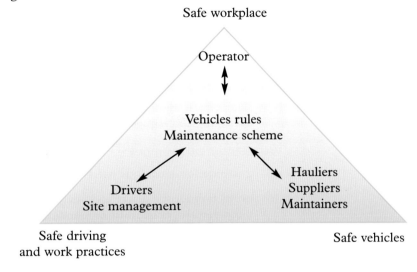

Figure 7 Responsibilities for ensuring safe operation of vehicles

2   Key elements in improving vehicle safety are:

(a)   designing the workplace to minimise the hazards;

(b)   using vehicles which are suitable, and well-maintained; and

(c)   establishing and following safe driving and working practices.

3   These issues can only be addressed if all parties involved co-operate in identifying and controlling the hazards involved.

4   The following guidance about vehicle safety is mainly based on the requirements of the Workplace (Health, Safety and Welfare) Regulations 1992 (the Workplace Regulations) and the Provision and Use of Work Equipment Regulations 1998 (PUWER), not the Quarries Regulations 1999. It is included here because it is particularly important in quarries and relevant to the vehicles rules in regulation 14.

5   The guidance is loosely organised into the three topics shown in Figure 7:

(a)   safe vehicles;

(b)   safe workplace; and

(c)   safe practices.

Safe vehicles

Suitability (PUWER - regulations 4 and 10)

6   Vehicles must be suitable for the place in which they are to be used and for the work they undertake. Principles of safe design for vehicles used in the extractive industries are set down in the Supply of Machinery (Safety) Regulations 1992 (Schedule 3, Parts 1 and 3).[33]

7   The selection of suitable work equipment can reduce or eliminate many risks at the quarry. It is generally much easier and cheaper to start with the right equipment than to modify it later. The following are important factors to consider when choosing a vehicle:

(a)   the effectiveness of the braking system, bearing in mind the slopes it is expected to work on;

(b)   adequate all-round visibility for the driver;

(c)   stability under all foreseeable operating conditions;

(d)   protection for the driver and any passengers from falling objects (falling object protective structures) and overturning (roll-over protective structures and seat belts);

(e)   safe access to and from the cab and other areas of the vehicle to which access may be required;

(f)   lights, windscreen wipers, horn and other warning devices;

(g)   guarding for dangerous parts during use or maintenance work;

(h)   protection for the driver and any passengers from rain, high and low temperatures, noise, dust or vibration; and

(i)   suitable seating for the driver and any passengers.

Visibility* (PUWER - regulations 5, 17 and 28)

8   To manoeuvre safely the driver needs to be able to see all around the vehicle or to be automatically warned if there is a person or object in the danger area. Vehicles should be designed to provide adequate visibility and be fitted with windows (including side windows), mirrors, closed-circuit TV and sensing equipment as appropriate.

9   Many vehicles have substantial blindspots, not only immediately behind the vehicle, but also alongside and immediately in front of it. Accidents occur when vehicles move off or turn while a pedestrian or vehicle is passing in a blindspot. How to avoid these blindspots is illustrated in Figure 8.

* See also Supply of Machinery (Safety) Regulations 1992, Schedule 3, paragraph 3.2.1.

Figure 8 Photo montage of a large dumper truck fitted with CCTV and mirrors to improve visibility from the driving position

10   Even when the driver's visibility is considered adequate, pedestrians should, so far as is reasonably practicable, be kept out of the area where vehicles operate (see paragraph 18 of this appendix).

11   Significantly smaller vehicles may be at risk of being crushed. Like pedestrians, they should ideally be kept away from areas where large vehicles operate. If this can not be achieved, they should be painted with distinctive colours, fitted with flashing lights or otherwise made readily visible to drivers of other vehicles.

Seat belts (PUWER - regulation 26)

12   Many injuries are the result of vehicles overturning. All drivers should therefore wear appropriate seat belts, preferably with a full harness, as should passengers when reasonably practicable. Road vehicles which are not provided with seat belts should not be allowed to enter areas where there is a significant risk of overturning.

Seats

13   Vehicle seats should be designed, maintained and adjusted to minimise the adverse effects of whole-body vibration on the driver, particularly where vehicles are used on rough terrain.

Brake testing

14   A suitable inspection scheme should be in place to ensure that brakes are in good condition at all times. This is often combined with other maintenance work.*

Tipping bodies

15   Vehicles should be fitted with devices to prevent tipping bodies accidentally collapsing from the raised position during maintenance. It is useful to put a notice on the vehicle to reinforce the use of the devices. Raised body alarms can reduce the risk of vehicles being driven 'tipped' and striking obstructions.

Safe workplace

Traffic routes (Workplace Regulations - regulation 17)

16   Roads and haulways must be safe as required by regulation 13 of the Quarries Regulations 1999. Traffic routes must be organised and suitably marked, for example by placing clear signs as required. Routes including one-way systems, which minimise reversing, are preferred.

17   Drivers who are not familiar with the site need to be given clear directions and, possibly, a map of the site showing their destination.

Pedestrian safety† (Workplace Regulations - regulation 17)

18   Pedestrians need to be kept away from vehicles, particularly where they have to reverse. They should use separate traffic routes wherever possible, for example pedestrian-only areas and safe, designated pedestrian routes.

---

* Quarries National Joint Advisory Committee *Guidance Note on brake testing schemes*. This is available from EPIC (see Appendix 6 for address). See also regulation 12 regarding inspection.

† See also the guide to the HSW Act (ISBN 0 7176 0441 1); section 2 in *Safe use of work equipment* (the PUWER guidance and ACOP, ISBN 0 7176 1626 6) paragraph 45; and regulation 4 of the Personal Protective Equipment at Work Regulations 1992.

Where this is not possible, high-visibility clothing★ and good lighting reduce the risks, as do the other requirements relating to speed, reversing and visibility referred to in this section.

Public safety

19   Where site vehicles cross a footpath or turn onto a public highway, particular consideration needs to be given to safeguarding the public. This may involve discussions with the planning, highway or police authority. The Road Traffic Act 1988, as amended, is the primary legislation for vehicles on the public highway.

Overhead power lines

20   Overhead power lines (see regulation 14 of the Electricity at Work Regulations 1989) on a site are likely to pose a significant risk, unless vehicles can not approach them. Vehicles do not need to strike the overhead lines for injury to occur - electricity can arc through a surprising distance depending on the voltage and conditions.

21   Precautions such as those illustrated in Figure 9 are required if it is possible for a vehicle to reach the danger zone around the cables. Assessment of the risk must take account of the possibility of tipper lorries travelling when tipped.

22   If work needs to be carried out below power lines and it is possible that cranes, excavators or other vehicles, could reach into the danger zone, the lines should normally be isolated and earthed before work begins. If this is not feasible, physical safeguards such as chains on the booms may be required to prevent vehicles reaching into the danger area.

23   Additional guidance may be found in GS6.[34] If in doubt, advice should be obtained from the electricity company.

★ Class 3 protective clothing. See BS EN 471[35] for further information.

Figure 9 Overhead cable protection on a vehicle traffic route

Safe practices

Drivers of vehicles (PUWER - regulation 9)

24   Regulation 9 of the Quarries Regulations 1999 and regulation 9 of
PUWER require drivers to be properly trained and competent. To operate
vehicles, drivers need to be authorised, in writing, by an appropriate manager
or supervisor. Training should be given by a suitable, competent person and
the need for refresher training should be considered.

25   The training required is not limited to the operation of the vehicle; it also
needs to cover the hazards related to its use in the workplace and the way
these are controlled, for example by the vehicles rules.

Speed of vehicles (Workplace Regulations - regulation 17)

26   The speed of vehicles should be appropriate for the conditions on the
site. Different speed limits may be needed in different parts of the quarry.
These limits should be indicated by suitable signs.

Reversing (Workplace Regulations - regulation 17)

27   Reversing is notoriously dangerous, particularly in confined areas such as
around hoppers and other plant, coaling sites, on benches and tips. The risk
involved can be reduced by:

(a)   minimising the need for reversing by the use of one-way systems and
turning areas;

(b)   ensuring adequate visibility for the driver;

(c)   providing safe systems of work; and

(d)   providing adequate supervision and training.

28   In areas where reversing is unavoidable, there must be effective
arrangements to ensure that it is safe to reverse every time. To reverse safely
the driver needs to be able to see the danger area at the rear of the vehicle, or
receive automatic warnings of any obstruction. The area must be clear of
pedestrians and other vehicles when reversing takes place.

29   Where safe reversing relies on reversing aids, for example closed-circuit
television or radar, the vehicle should not be used if the devices are defective.

30   When it is dark, the site lighting and vehicle lights should provide
sufficient illumination for the driver to see clearly when reversing.

31   No single safeguard is likely to be sufficient on its own during reversing.
All the relevant precautions need to be considered together (see Table 4).

Road vehicles

32   Road vehicles are subject to PUWER if they are used at work, whether
exclusively or not. This includes all quarry vehicles, including those operated
by haulage companies, which are used on public roads, except for purely
private vehicles. Road traffic legislation normally takes precedence when these
vehicles are used off-site.

85

33   If the on-site risk is the same as when a vehicle is used on public roads then additional safeguards are unlikely to be needed. If, however, the risk is different or greater because of the way a vehicle is used or because of site conditions, additional precautions may be required. In such cases this should be covered in the vehicle rules produced in accordance with regulation 14.

34   Where additional safeguards are proposed for road vehicles, they must also comply with the requirements of the Road Vehicles (Construction and Use) Regulations 1986.

Table 4 Control measures for reversing operations

Eliminate need to reverse	Implement one-way systems around site and in loading and unloading areas Provide designated turning areas
Reduce reversing operations	Reduce the number of vehicle movements as far as possible Instruct drivers not to reverse, unless absolutely necessary
Ensure adequate visibility for drivers	Fit CCTV, radar, convex mirrors etc to overcome restrictions to visibility from the driver's seat, particularly at the sides and rear of vehicles
Ensure safe systems of work are followed	Design vehicle reversing areas which: • allow adequate space for vehicles to manoeuvre safely; • exclude pedestrians; • are clearly signed; and • have suitable physical stops, eg bunds of material or buffers, to warn drivers that they have reached the limit of the safe reversing area Ensure everyone on site understands the vehicles rules Ensure all vehicles on site are fitted with appropriate warning devices **Check that procedures work in practice, and are actually being followed**

Legislation relevant to transport in quarries

Provision and Use of Work Equipment Regulations 1998

Suitability of work equipment

PUWER

4

(1)   Every employer shall ensure that work equipment is so constructed or adapted as to be suitable for the purpose for which it is used or provided.

(2)   In selecting work equipment, every employer shall have regard to the working conditions and to the risks to the health and safety of persons which exist in the premises or undertaking in which that work equipment is to be used and any additional risk posed by the use of that work equipment.

(3)   Every employer shall ensure that work equipment is used only for operations for which, and under conditions for which, it is suitable.

(4)   In this regulation "suitable" means suitable in any respect which it is reasonably foreseeable will affect the health or safety of any person.

Maintenance

PUWER
5

(1)   Every employer shall ensure that work equipment is maintained in an efficient state, in efficient working order and in good repair.

Controls

PUWER

17

(1)   Every employer shall ensure that all controls for work equipment are clearly visible and identifiable, including by appropriate marking where necessary.

(3)   Every employer shall ensure where appropriate -

(a)   that, so far as is reasonably practicable, the operator of any control is able to ensure from the position of that control that no person is in a place where he would be exposed to any risk to his health or safety as a result of the operation of that control, but where or to the extent that it is not reasonably practicable;

(b)   that, so far as is reasonably practicable, systems of work are effective to ensure that, when work equipment is about to start, no person is in a place where he would be exposed to a risk to his health or safety as a result of the work equipment starting, but where neither of these is reasonably practicable;

(c)   that an audible, visible or other suitable warning is given by virtue of regulation 24 whenever work equipment is about to start.

(4)   Every employer shall take appropriate measures to ensure that any person who is in a place where he would be exposed to a risk to his health or safety as a result of the starting or stopping of work equipment has sufficient time and suitable means to avoid that risk.

Regulation 25 — Employees carried on mobile work equipment

PUWER

25

Every employer shall ensure that no employee is carried by mobile work equipment unless -

(a)   it is suitable for carrying persons; and

(b)   it incorporates features for reducing to as low as is reasonably practicable risks to their safety, including risks from wheels or tracks.

Regulation 26 — Rolling over of mobile work equipment

PUWER

26

(1)   Every employer shall ensure that where there is a risk to an employee riding on mobile work equipment from its rolling over, it is minimised by -

(a)   stabilising the work equipment;

(b)   a structure which ensures that the work equipment does no more than fall on its side;

(c)   a structure giving sufficient clearance to anyone being carried if it overturns further than that; or

(d)   a device giving comparable protection.

(2)   Where there is a risk of anyone being carried by mobile work equipment being crushed by its rolling over, the employer shall ensure that it has a suitable restraining system for him.

(3)   This regulation shall not apply to a fork-lift truck having a structure described in sub-paragraph (b) or (c) of paragraph (1).

(4)   Compliance with this regulation is not required where -

(a)   it would increase the overall risk to safety;

(b)   it would not be reasonably practicable to operate the mobile work equipment in consequence; or

(c)   in relation to an item of work equipment provided for use in the undertaking or establishment before 5th December 1998 it would not be reasonably practicable.

Regulation 28 — Self-propelled work equipment

PUWER

28

Every employer shall ensure that, where self-propelled work equipment may, while in motion, involve risk to the safety of persons -

(a)   it has facilities for preventing its being started by an unauthorised person;

(b)   it has appropriate facilities for minimising the consequences of a collision where there is more than one item of rail-mounted work equipment in motion at the same time;

(c)   it has a device for braking and stopping;

(d) where safety constraints so require, emergency facilities operated by readily accessible controls or automatic systems are available for braking and stopping the work equipment in the event of failure of the main facility;

(e) where the driver's direct field of vision is inadequate to ensure safety, there are adequate devices for improving his vision so far as is reasonably practicable;

(f) if provided for use at night or in dark places -

(i) it is equipped with lighting appropriate to the work to be carried out; and

(ii) is otherwise sufficiently safe for such use;

(g) if it, or anything carried or towed by it, constitutes a fire hazard and is liable to endanger employees, it carries appropriate fire-fighting equipment, unless such equipment is kept sufficiently close to it.

Workplace (Health, Safety and Welfare) Regulations 1992

Organisation etc of traffic routes

(1) Every workplace shall be organised in such a way that pedestrians and vehicles can circulate in a safe manner.

(2) Traffic routes in a workplace shall be suitable for the persons or vehicles using them, sufficient in number, in suitable positions and of sufficient size.

(3) Without prejudice to the generality of paragraph (2), traffic routes shall not satisfy the requirements of that paragraph unless suitable measures are taken to ensure that -

(a) pedestrians or, as the case may be, vehicles may use a traffic route without causing danger to the health or safety of persons at work near it;

(b) there is sufficient separation of any traffic route for vehicles from doors or gates or from traffic routes for pedestrians which lead onto it; and

(c) where vehicles and pedestrians use the same traffic route, there is sufficient separation between them.

(4) All traffic routes shall be suitably indicated where necessary for reasons of health or safety.

(5) Paragraph (2) shall apply so far as is reasonably practicable, to a workplace which is not a new workplace, a modification, an extension or a conversion.

Appendix 6	**Useful addresses**

ABMEC (Association of British Mining
Equipment Companies)
Henley Grove Road
Rotherham
Yorkshire S61 1LZ

Tel: 01709 555402
Fax: 01709 555758
e-mail: deakin@abmec.org.uk.

British Ball Clay Producers Association
Park House
Courtenay Park
Newton Abbot
Devon TQ12 4PS

Tel: 01626 332345
Fax: 01626 332344
e-mail: cwatts@wbb.co.uk.

British Drilling Association
Wayside
London End
Upper Boddington
Daventry
Northants NN11 6DP

Tel: 01327 264622
Fax: 01327 264623
e-mail: none

The British Cement Association
Century House
Telford Avenue
Crowthorne
Berkshire RG45 6YS

Tel: 01344 762676
Fax: 01344 727205
e-mail: kbrogan@bca.org.uk

The British Ceramic Confederation
Federation House
Station Road
Stoke-on-Trent
Staffordshire ST4 2SA

Tel: 01782 744631
Fax: 01782 744102
e-mail: bcc@ceramfed.co.uk.

China Clay Association
John Keay House
St Austell
Cornwall PL25 4DJ

Tel: 01726 74482
Fax: 01726 623019
e-mail: trish.dotjones@ecci.co.uk

COALPRO
Confederation House
Thornes Office Park
Denby Dale Road
Wakefield
Yorkshire WF2 7AN

Tel: 01924 200802
Fax: 01924 200796
e-mail: anna@coalpro.demon.co.uk.

Environmental Services Association
154 Buckingham Palace Road
London SW1W 9TR

Tel: 020 7824 8882
Fax: 020 7824 8753
e-mail: info@esauk.org

EPIC
Ground Floor Suite
Longmire House
36/38 London Road
St Albans
Hertfordshire AL1 1NG

Tel: 01727 869008
Fax: 01727 843318
e-mail: epicnto@aol.com